"We are all players in the game of life . . . and this book shows you how to be a winner. Barry Neil Kaufman's new book champions making the choice to believe in ourselves, to have a positive attitude, to be hopeful and to seize the power of loving ourselves and others."

—Lou Holtz
Head Football Coach
University of Notre Dame

"For those who sincerely want to follow the supreme law of love, Barry Kaufman's book provides an unexpected blueprint to selfless living."

—Father John Catoir
Director, The Christophers

"Within these pages Kaufman unfolds a precious secret for attaining happiness and leading a more meaningful, joyful life. . . . A wonderfully wise, warm and insightful book that is sure to reward those who read it with a richer, more balanced life."

—Jesse Stoff, M.D.
Author of *The Chronic Fatigue Syndrome*

"Barry Neil Kaufman has written a moving exploration of the healing power of compassion and caring. *Happiness Is a Choice* affirms the unlimited potential of the human spirit and offers hope to those who have been challenged by adversity."

—Coretta Scott King
Founding President/CEO
The Martin Luther King, Jr., Center
for Nonviolent Social Change

Happiness
Is a Choice

BARRY NEIL KAUFMAN

Fawcett   New York

A Fawcett Book
Published by The Random House Publishing Group

Published in the United States by Ballantine Books, an imprint of The Random House Publishing Group, a division of Random House, Inc., New York, and simultaneously in Canada by Random House of Canada Limited, Toronto.

Library of Congress Catalog Card Number: 92-90383

Fawcett is a registered trademark and the Fawcett colophon is a trademark of Random House, Inc.

www.ballantinebooks.com

ISBN 0-449-90799-6

Cover design by Judy Herbstman

Manufactured in the United States of America

First Ballantine Books Trade Paperback Edition: January 1994

29 28 27 26 25 24 23 22

Unhappiness is not inevitable.

Even when we are angry, judgmental and miserable,
we have the best of intentions.

We have been systematically taught to use discomfort
as a strategy to take care of ourselves.

We can un-teach ourselves . . . and begin again.

*

Unhappiness is not an enemy—just a choice.

This book is not based on a moral imperative:
no shoulds or should nots, just choices.

*

When we choose happiness,
we choose love and inner peace.

When we choose love and inner peace,
we help others on the planet choose it as well
. . . by our example.

*   *   *

We can live our dreams . . . instead of just dreaming them.

We can make a difference!

We ARE the difference.

Contents

Acknowledgments/Gratitude

Rather than simply respond or react, I have learned to initiate and create many events in my life. I have also learned to take charge of my internal process and design my responses to the many unpredictable circumstances which greeted me along the way. In the last twenty years, I have come to view most of these opportunities as celebrations; some as struggles. I did the best I could, like all of us, and although I might choose to handle myself differently if the universe gave me a second opportunity with certain circumstances, I find myself greeting each new day with no regrets or embarrassment. The overwhelming sensation I feel is one of gratitude for those who have and continue to support my wife and me in our work with others.

Although we could never claim perfection in our pursuit of a happier lifestyle, we stretched ourselves continually and passionately to live more fully with a clear and prioritized intention. Then we were blessed again and again when those who came initially as strangers to our teaching center stayed for training, and then joined us to help reach out to others and create an amazingly open and loving extended family. This book reflects the possibilities that bubbled forth from that coming together which allowed us to design a sweet, supportive and challenging human laboratory where prioritizing the pursuit of happiness could be actualized. We wanted to demonstrate that personal exploration and personal growth could not only be easy, but could also be an exciting adventure. Thus, documented throughout these pages are the stories, struggles and triumphs of the many ordinary people who took giant steps in their own lives. Their giant steps rest on the shoulders of a very special and dedicated group of people.

A deep, resounding sense of appreciation for Steven and Gita Wertz, who dared to hold the torch of hope and possibility with my wife and me by joining us wholeheartedly in teaching happiness and love and working with children and families who had been given no hope. They helped make a dream and this book possible. Words can barely express the impact on my life and on the pages of this book by Bonnie

Pfeiffer and Anne Bianchi, who have championed "going for the gold" and lavishly supported me with their love, friendship and tireless energy. My personal assistant, Kirsten Jones, tickled me daily with her childlike enthusiasm, her deep delight and unending love. She made direct contributions to supporting this effort with research and nitty-gritty input for which I will be forever grateful. Darlene Love (that's her real name) gave me evenings and weekends for months to assist in typing, retyping and loving each page to life. Warm thanks to Margaret Boydstun, who helped me fine-tune sentences, paragraphs and chapters so that I could better express what I wanted to share. I much appreciate her sensitivity, skill, enthusiasm and caring.

There are others who have lent their support and contributed directly and/or indirectly in the adventures and insights shared in this book: Melany Kahn and Antonette "Toni" Badami's love for this process turned into a whirlwind passion that spread these ideas throughout the country and inspired countless numbers of people to change their lives; Bryn Kaufman Hogan, who began this journey as a child trying to help her once-autistic brother, made her joy in what we teach a wondrous invitation for so many families, children and individuals to dare to find the best in themselves; Gary Skow held out his hand in love and mentored some of the people who appear on the pages of this book, and my gratitude to Jennifer Hanson, Gerd Winkler, Mecki Augustin, Jim

Stevenson, Susan Abrams, Matt Koehler, Ginger Block, William Hogan, Bonnie Knight, Lorenzo Lydon, Laura Putts-Galinas, Ken and Janet Hudonjorgenson, Kathleen Sullivan, Ebo Teichmann, Nancy Judson, Najda Noonan, as well as Joan Crager, Laura Plunkett, Linda Weltner, Rob Johnstone, Chuck Blevins, Daniel Ladouceur and Murielle Matteau-Ladouceur, Real Choiniere and Jocelyna Dubuc, Marcia Goldman, Cordelia Shaw, Liz Dickinson, Elizabeth Shulman, Jeanne Coleman, Jane and Tom Welch, Nancy and Eric Suhadolc, Batya and Jordan Yasgur, Dorene Pontikes, Connie Packard, Jeri Pugh and a host of others who have had a most meaningful impact in reaching out and making their love tangible.

This acknowledgment list would certainly not be complete without the inspiration of all those families who have come to The Option Institute and Fellowship (our teaching center) and continue to try with courage, daring, dedication, enthusiasm and love to help their special children reach for the stars. They are the heroes: Pat and Grant Tyler, Connie and Akhtar Kahn, Koby and Rozzie Feldman, Shelly Allen, Patty and Paul Fiske, Barbara and Bo Waite, Pauline and Richard Banducci, Frank and Kathy Almeida, Donna and Mike Basich, Lynne and Tom Caiafa, Janine and Scott Fisher, Seerat and Earnest Emmanuel, Shaya and Leah Nebenzahl, Sarah and Peter Hamilton-Ely, Gayle and Neland Nobel—just to name a few of the families who, indeed, have chosen to make a difference!

My thanks and love to all those people who have come to learn, do sessions, participate in our programs and share the most intimate details of their lives in an effort to find happier, more loving and humane solutions to their situations. Their journeys helped blaze the trail. To my parents, Abe and Roz, whose abiding love and dedication to family I always appreciate.

If a book could be said to have an ultimate sponsor, this one had my wife and life partner, Samahria, who enriched each page with her caring, her savvy, her love of me and so many around her. As I write, she's not close to my heart . . . she's in my heart.

All of these people have been gifts in my life. I feel honored to have their support and grateful for what I have learned from each of them.

Author's additional note: Frequently, I use stories of actual events and experiences to illustrate points and possibilities. In many cases, names of people, places and details have been changed to protect the privacy of those involved. In addition, some references to mind-stretching experiments and theories in science and medicine are introduced as hors d'oeuvres of delight in a simple and easily digestible fashion to assist the reader in playing further with the ideas and opportunities presented throughout these pages. For those wanting specific names and other details, a reference section has been provided at the end of the book.

In appreciation, Barry ("Bears") Neil Kaufman

c/o Option Institute
P.O. Box 1180-H
Sheffield, MA 01257
(413) 229-2100

Happiness
Is a Choice

Personal Note

Years ago, following the publication of my first book about the uplifting journey my family took to heal our special child (once neurologically impaired and dysfunctioning), I spoke with a man who had written quite a different saga. He documented what he experienced as the difficult and damning reality of parenting a "less-than-perfect" youngster. He declared without apology that he hated people like me.

"You take something that's terrible," he said flatly, "and make believe it's beautiful."

I considered his point of view for a moment. "Did you ever consider," I asked softly, "that you might be taking something that's beautiful and making believe it's terrible?"

At that moment, I realized that neither one of us held the truth, only a vision we had each created and then used to embrace our situation. I had decided to see my son and his difficulties as an opportunity to grow, learn and love. He regarded his situation as a curse. Our different experiences had followed from those distinctly different visions.

Wanting to reach out to him, I told him that I, too, would have once been overwhelmed and devastated by such an event. I remember, in grade school, watching a group of mentally retarded students trying to master the simplest aspects of a baseball game without success. I turned away, confused and uncomfortable about what I had witnessed. In high school, a boy in one of my classes walked with a limp, his left hand and arm contorted awkwardly. When he tried to speak, he had tremendous difficulty forming words and drooled uncontrollably each time he labored to verbalize even the shortest sentence. The teacher told us that Douglas had been born that way. Sometimes, other students mimicked his movements and laughed at their pantomimes. For one semester I tried to help him by carrying his bookbag, though I felt somewhat awkward, embarrassed and scared each time. I never knew what to say to him, so we walked together from the bus to the school building in silence.

Before the arrival of our first child, I thought about Douglas and how his life seemed like torture to me. I remember lying in bed one night, staring at the huge abdomen of my pregnant wife and thinking, "Oh God, what if . . . just what if what happened to Douglas happened to us and our child?" I remember praying for a healthy baby. Indeed, our first two children, both daughters, arrived as healthy and energetic little people. Our third child was very different. However, by the time of his arrival, my wife and I both had changed dramatically from the frightened and uncomfortable people who had greeted those first years of marriage and child rearing.

I tried to explain how the world had changed for me, in significant and irrevocable ways, once I had changed my own vision of life and had begun to make happiness and love priorities. As a result, my wife and I could greet our special child as a wonderful opportunity. The man with the different point of view listened to my sharing without comment. Finally, he laughed at my unending enthusiasm. He decided I had been well-intentioned but, nonetheless, naive and unrealistic in my hopefulness and happiness. He questioned the validity of my attitude. Ultimately, he preferred what he called his sanity.

The way we choose to see the world creates the world we see.

During a question-and-answer segment immediately following a class I had conducted on developing attitudes of self-trust, a participant raised his hand tentatively. When I nodded at him, he withdrew at first, then leaned forward cautiously.

"My question is, um, somewhat related to what we've discussed, but in a bit of a different direction, and, er, more personal. I am having so much trouble with my asthma. I've gone from doctor to doctor. I take all the medication they've prescribed, but nothing really helps. I just can't stand it. I wonder if you could say something, well, anything, that might be useful."

I hesitated for a moment and considered sharing with him several scientific studies that would lay a foundation for what I knew would be my answer. However, the class had only minutes left. Finally, I smiled broadly and said, "This may sound silly or crazy or both, but I'll do my best to give you a useful response. Be happy with your asthma! Instead of treating it like an enemy, embrace it like a friend. If you change your attitude about your condition you'll change the chemistry in your body. Every thought we have is a physical event. Neurotransmitters and neuropeptides pop into existence throughout the body each time we activate a belief. Change the belief (the thought, the perspective, the judgment) and we change or, at the very least, influence the physical event we call our 'bodymind.' Your attitude and intelligence exist everywhere in the 50 trillion cells of your body. This is a marvelous and concrete opportunity for you, not just a pie-in-the-sky game. Give yourself and your asthma a different message and see what happens. So, when you have the tightness in your chest, the shortness of breath, the wheezing or coughing, you could first welcome it, talk to it, even play with it. Then open yourself, ultimately, to loving it . . . really loving it!"

He seemed amused, intrigued and skeptical. "I thought you'd say something like that," he replied, chuckling. "Well, what do I have to lose? Okay, I'll try it."

The very next day, he came to the morning session of the program visibly rested and alert. "I had a special experience last night," he told the group. "I greeted my nightly wheezing with a smile instead of my usual annoyance or depression. I actually did say hello out loud and laughed. I talked to my asthma like a friend. Wow! I told my asthma, we sure have a lot of history together." He smiled shyly, then continued, "I even thanked my bronchial tubes each time I coughed. At first, I felt . . . well, absolutely ridiculous, but soon something magically freed up inside and I really felt loving and loved." His eyes filled with tears. "You know, in no time at all, I fell asleep. Right now, I feel more comfortable and peaceful in my body than I have in months."

This man had eased himself into being happy and loving toward a condition he had previously viewed as intolerable.

He had created a powerful attitudinal advantage for himself. His play, his talk and his laughter helped him to change his vision of asthma from enemy to friend, and his new vision in turn changed his experience.

Each of us can, in a simple and easy way, access an amazing attitudinal advantage within ourselves once we come to know that happiness (and love) is a choice and misery is optional (not inevitable).

I never knew I could just claim happiness, at any time, as my birthright and not be limited by the condemning evidence of my own personal history and the past. That awareness, which I previously resisted as preposterous, has been a blessing and changed my life profoundly, allowing me in my own imperfect way to be so much more loving, peaceful and useful to myself and all those I touch.

During this past summer (as in many previous summers), my teaching staff and I lived and worked for two full months with a group of forty-two adults who had come together as strangers for eight weeks to form what became an instant family. This diverse group included a physician, a farmer, a lawyer, a social worker, homemakers, an engineer, a psychotherapist, a nurse, an artist, a carpenter, an actress, a computer programmer, a textile designer, several business executives, some entrepreneurs, teachers, college students, retirees and the like. They ranged in age from late teens to mid-seventies and hailed from urban and rural centers across the United States as well as from other countries. Together, we created an intention to explore completely the very substances of who we were and to recreate ourselves in accordance with our own individual designs. We dared to experiment with ourselves and then to live in ways that others might easily dismiss as "unrealistic" or "impossible." Ultimately, the members of this amazing group ("amazing" tends to be my consistent reflection about all the groups, families and individuals I have had the privilege to facilitate) resourced and taught each other, crashed through the walls of limiting beliefs and constructed what we called "a vision to live by."

Each day we gathered together for experiential interactions, discussions, intimate sharings and segments for self-exploration. We laughed. We cried. We shouted. We whispered. We challenged each other. We loved and hugged each other. Eventually, we forged a respectful and honoring family of dear and supportive friends. Finally, we turned to an easel at the front of our meeting room and composed guidelines for an intentional lifestyle and then, in the weeks that followed, we put those guidelines into action with great energy and enthusiasm. We not only created a prototype of interfacing with other people in a happy, loving, accepting, stimulating and harmonious way, but also re-created our personal belief systems so we could be continuously open, self-accepting, energetic, embracing, joyful and yet unflappable (not vulnerable) in the face of judgments and criticism of others.

Even though we tripped and stumbled over old beliefs and judgments at times, we could not contain our awe and delight in what we had accomplished. No one could ever take that experience and learning from us or diminish the inspiration of what could become a possibility for everyday living on this planet. We did more than just dream that dream . . . we lived it, challenging and tickling each other until everyone had endless opportunities to experience their own momentous changes.

In response to their own appreciation for creating rapid, even instant, change in themselves, some members of this group returned to our teaching center (as did members of similar groups before them) with their entire families and helped loved ones quickly establish more open, intimate, supportive and loving relationships. Others brought friends and coworkers who wanted easier, sweeter and more nurturing life experiences and were willing to experiment by translating what they wanted into action. One man came back with the key executives from his company for a special program designed to help them create and live a common intention which encouraged open, authentic, energetic, creative and fearless interaction.

"A vision to live by" has not only become the backbone for the staff and volunteers at our teaching center, but also the wellspring of inspiration for the individuals, families and groups we teach as well as an essential frame of reference for this book.

We now witness people implementing in hours what took us years to understand. The ideas contained on these pages can become a simple blueprint into which anyone can breathe life and thereby make profound, immediate changes. Oftentimes, we limit our perspective to past references, citing the evidence of yesterday as proof of what's possible. But evidence tells us nothing about what we can be and do if we choose to walk a different path. When we have mentored people confronting catastrophic illnesses or situations and watched them triumph, defying the statistics and the predictions of experts, we are awestruck by people's ability to reclaim their personal power and sense of self-trust. Suddenly, anything seems possible.

Now I would like to take your hand and guide you through a few hours of reading which, I believe, will enable you to make the most important decision of your life . . . to seize an attitudinal advantage by becoming happy and more loving right now, this instant, whatever your circumstances.

Remember, as you read, there will be something to decide and something to do . . . an easy, but amazing adventure.

I · Living the Dream

To no longer simply believe in what is,
but to start to believe in what you want.

BNK

For twenty years, my wife and I have devoted ourselves single-mindedly to a very focused, yet simple pursuit, so simple as to seem unworthy. The pursuit of happiness!

Prior to that endeavor, we muddled through our days with no clear path to travel. We wanted to make happiness and love the basis of our relationship but felt incapable of bringing them to life. The dream had no form. The inspiration faded like a childhood song whose tune we could hum but whose words we had forgotten.

Like those around us, we lived with our everyday fears, anger, anxiety, impatience and distrust. Yet, simultaneously, we searched for a philosophy, psychology or spiritual connection which might enable us to make sense out of our lives and resolve the doubts and dissatisfactions that plagued us. The beautiful and, at times, exhausting journey through books, graduate courses in philosophy and psychology, seminars in comparative religion and cross-cultural studies, psychodynamic training workshops, meditative retreats, as well as personal analysis and individual tutorials yielded separate pieces of a puzzle that, unfortunately, never came together as a whole.

Finally, we learned to investigate the inner university of our beliefs and feelings through gentle, nondirective, eye-opening questions. Over time, we used these dialogues to explore every aspect of ourselves. Nothing escaped our scrutiny. Slowly, we began to trust our own inner direction and value our own natural expertise. We chose, as our daily intention, a happier and more loving embrace of ourselves and those around us. We began to let go of our judgments of people and events and came to see our lives through new and increasingly optimistic eyes.

Happiness no longer eluded us; it became the child of our choices and decisions. So awesomely simple! Rather than become passive as our happiness grew, we became more energized, more resourceful than ever before and more capable of translating our ideas into actions. Certainly, we were anything but perfect in our understanding, yet soon we would apply this unfolding awareness as a profound and powerful attitudinal advantage in a host of situations.

Our pursuit of happiness and the actuality of becoming happier empowered us more than we had ever anticipated. We could say easily that living more happily and teaching others to do the same certainly feels good . . . and that would be reason enough to pursue it and teach it. But we never foresaw how transforming and practical a happy and loving attitude could be in facing the big and little challenges of everyday living. Though readers of my other books might be familiar with the following story, I want to share it here briefly because it demonstrates one of many miracles that have come from being happier and also footnotes a key turning point in our lives that led my wife and me, ultimately, to the substance shared in this book.

Our third child, our first son, had been diagnosed at eighteen months of age as suffering from a supposedly incurable neurological and brain disorder called autism. He spent his waking hours spinning in circles, rocking back and forth, flapping his fingers in front of his eyes and making an endless series of strange, sometimes eerie, sounds. Inanimate objects such as wood blocks, shoelaces, crinkled paper and dinner plates consumed his attention hypnotically, leaving his world devoid of sustained and intimate human contact. When we lifted him or cuddled him in our arms, he became limp, dangling lifelessly like a rag doll. He never quite looked at us, but peered through us, his eyes fixed and unresponsive. We stood outside his silent alien universe, wanting passionately to find the doorway in.

As physicians and neuropsychologists shook their heads with obvious sympathy, we reaffirmed, as best we could, the happier, nonjudgmental life perspective we had adopted which enabled us now to embrace our very unusual child in awe and appreciation. As they detailed his profound deficiencies, we noted his flickering abilities. When they encouraged institutionalization, we suggested love. When they advised realism, we countered with hope. These experts declared the situation unchangeable and our little boy forever unreachable. According to their prognosis, he would never talk or communicate normally and would be lost forever behind a wall of bizarre and potentially self-destructive behaviors.

Maybe some of you have experienced a situation in which a loved one was desperately or terminally ill, or a circumstance in which a child or friend suffered from pain even the doctors could not take away. Maybe when you could not find a source of support or hope in any person or any service on earth, you did what we did. We turned to God more fervently than ever and drew upon that special connection in order to understand and find inspiration to deal with this challenging, mystifying and traumatic illness that had engulfed our son.

For my wife and me, questioning ourselves and looking inside for a deeper grasp of our faith helped us crystallize even more clearly the nature of communion; namely, it was one of happiness, love, peace and acceptance. Those very principles which we had already been incorporating into our daily living process would now guide us more emphatically than ever. We defied both the medical and educational professionals who damned our son as hopeless and took the first steps toward designing our own home-based program for our very, very special child.

We began to do what others judged to be nonsense. We decided to be happy with our son and rather than push him to come to us and conform to our world (which appeared outside of his capability), we joined him in his. Since we did not judge his autistic behaviors as "bad" or "sick" but saw them as the best he could do for now, we used them as vehicles to communicate acceptance and to teach him about the world. When he rocked, we rocked with him. When he flapped his fingers, we flapped ours. When he spun plates on the floor, we spun plates with him. When he emitted high-pitched, warbling screeches, we learned his song and tried to sing it with him. We did not merely imitate him; we joined him fully, with great sincerity and enthusiasm. Slowly, we reached into the darkness and, by means of a massive stimulation program, built bridges of words and affection between us.

We turned our lives upside down. We altered the rooms in our home to accommodate the program and radically changed every family member's routine, balancing our work with our son carefully with special times set aside to nurture our young daughters. In turn, they both joined our efforts and became teachers for their own brother. Eventually, I left a successful business I had spent eight years building.

Every day became another opportunity to recommit ourselves to this journey. Above all, each moment became a concrete celebration of happiness as we played lovingly with our dysfunctioning son on a landscape that frightened so many others. By taking thousands of painstakingly tiny steps with him, we taught him how to speak, interact with people and master self-help skills that other children learn easily and quickly on their own.

After we had worked with him twelve hours a day, seven days a week for over three years, this mute, dysfunctioning, severely retarded, under-30 I.Q. autistic child blossomed into a highly verbal, extroverted, expressive and loving youngster, who bore absolutely no traces of his original condition. Raun went on to display a near-genius I.Q. and maintained an almost straight "A" academic average in both grade school and high school, graduating with honors. Currently, he attends one of the finest universities in the country, loves tennis, volleyball and cross-country skiing and lights up our home with his unending curiosity, wit and laughter.

Our work with our son became a life-changing milestone for us. We had created what we now consider was our first substantial religious experience, one characterized by a deep sense of communion, inner peace and acceptance. We wanted to re-create the essence of that experience, as best we could, in all the other facets of our lives: from driving in rush hour traffic to making love, from preparing a meal to helping our children with homework, from cleaning a floor to honoring the efforts of our parents. The implications dazzled us; the change in our lives could be monumental, making every event irrevocably different.

To our amazement, our journey with our son and his rebirth, recounted in my book *Son-Rise* and the network television movie of the same title, brought hundreds, then thousands, to our door. First came families with special children, then sons and daughters with desperately sick parents, then lovers and friends trying to help those turned away by the experts as hopeless. We insisted we could not guarantee that what had worked so wonderfully with our son and had transformed our own lives would remedy anyone else's situation. The responses came immediately. "We don't expect any promises, just hope. Teach us to love and to have hope."

For some who came, the inspiration of hope and happiness was enough; others wanted us to teach them how to uproot their discomforts and discard the beliefs which fueled them as their prerequisite for changing. My second book, *To*

Love Is to Be Happy With, fully explained the questions and the dialogue process that had transformed our lives and that we now teach. It became a handbook for people wanting to incorporate the attitude and principles of happiness, love and acceptance into their daily lives. We called what we shared The Option Process.® As more individuals and families came, we had endless opportunities to work with many who would profoundly enhance their relationships with lovers, friends and children, their careers, their health and their self-esteem by becoming happier. Some of our students wanted to take this attitude of happiness and love, which they had learned to make tangible, and reach out to those around them. As a result, we had the blessing to witness seemingly impossible events.

A mute child who had never spoken learned to talk. A young boy crippled by a progressive genetic disease started to use his hands after three years of disuse. After four suicide attempts, a young woman found a powerful way to reconnect with her life and her parents, clearly affirming life over death for the first time in ten years. A mother who had abandoned her children created a wellspring of love inside herself which enabled her to return and re-embrace her family. A woman, scarred over forty percent of her body by an explosion and fire, came to see the beauty in her physical form and no longer hid from those who chose to stare at her. A retired business-man stopped feeling useless and dedicated himself to learning a new profession. A couple took the "war" out of their relationship and found a tenderness for each other that they had never anticipated could exist. A father came to accept his schizophrenic daughter and, for the first time, pierced the wall of her apparent madness to discover a very coherent, love-starved child whom he could now embrace.

Since we predicated our work on being with adults, children and families with an accepting, nonjudgmental and loving attitude, we felt grateful to base our lives on a conscious design which gave us daily practice in happily embracing and honoring those around us. Certainly, we had and continue to have much to learn and a great eagerness to grow into the fullness of what we teach. It has been said that people instruct others in what they, themselves, want most to learn. That insight holds true for us. Every day, I am aware of my own studentship, perceiving myself as an excited apprentice who sees the art and wonder of the craft but has yet to master all the skills necessary to attain it. However, each day we learn more. The teaching becomes less an activity but more a lifestyle to live and to breathe.

Prompted by the requests of people searching for happier and more humane ways to deal with their doubts and difficulties, my wife and I wrote more books and, finally, in 1983, we founded The Option Institute and Fellowship, a learning center located in a pastoral mountain setting in western Massachusetts. Over the years, a group of dedicated men and women have joined hands with us to provide helpful, and at times life-saving, programs for thousands of individuals and families. Additionally, we have created together an informal community of people who support each other in our intention to be happier, more loving and more accepting of ourselves and others. We changed so much through these experiences that my wife changed her name from Suzi to Samahria (which means rebirth of the spirit) in order to more accurately reflect her changing self. I still retain the name of "Bears," given to me over twenty years ago as a playful commentary on my size, my bearded appearance and my bear hugs.

After participating in our son's rebirth and establishing of our learning center, we felt so happy and grateful that we wanted to make our happiness and gratitude even more tangible. As a celebration of that inspiration, we decided to adopt children others did not want.

Our first adopted child, Tayo, at one year of age, had been severely malnourished as well as weakened by dysentery and intestinal parasites. His head appeared enlarged, his liver distended and his rib cage flared. Initially he had difficulty lifting his head or rolling over and could not crawl. However, although he had been deprived of meaningful contact and affection throughout his short life, he had a big smile for anyone who looked his way. With the assistance of our other children, we worked to help this little boy overcome the deprivation of his early living experience. At first, as with our once autistic son, we had to teach him skills other children mastered easily. His spirited desire to learn challenged us to invent games and activities which would help him gain control over his limbs so he could crawl, climb and, ultimately, walk. We learned so much about the power of personal motivation from this little guy! Today Tayo is a lively and talented youngster who asks thousands of "why" questions and delights in expressing himself through his own highly original cartoon drawings. In addition, after each meal, he still checks out the proposed content and location of his next one as if to reassure himself in some deep place inside that he will not starve again.

A most significant learning came with the arrival of our second adopted child, a little boy we named Ravi, who had lived in a poverty-stricken area of Bogota, Colombia, and whose mother had died when he was three and a half years old. A month after her death, Ravi wandered into the kitchen of his meager hovel in search of food. He had not eaten that day. When he noticed his father cutting up slices of bananas and eating them, he asked for some pieces for himself. His father refused and muttered angrily. The little boy persisted. In a soft, pleading voice, he asked again for just one small bite. His father jumped from the table in fury with a cutting knife in hand and plunged it into his son's neck, then purposely slit his throat twice. Neighbors found the child soon after the attack and rushed him to a hospital where he miraculously survived. Since he had no living relatives to claim him after his father's arrest and subsequent imprisonment, local social service workers placed Ravi in an orphanage, where he languished for almost two years until one of the directors brought him to our attention. Though his vocal cords remained intact, he barely spoke and acted in ways which could be construed as justifiable signs of trauma and disturbance.

My father, upon hearing the news of this proposed adoption, called and asked pointedly, "Are you looking for more trouble?" A psychologist consulting on the home study (required by the stateside adoption process) warned that this little boy had been severely injured, physically, mentally and emotionally, and would show signs of that disabling trauma for the rest of his life. A friend raised issues about what kind of sacrifices would be necessary, especially so soon after we had just finished integrating Tayo into our family. I told them all that we could not honestly relate to those concerns. We have never knowingly invited trouble into our lives; we try, as best we can, to invite wonderful experiences. In addition, we believed, or at least were hopeful, that any child or adult could flourish in spite of having endured the most horrendous of circumstances. And finally, adopting this child has nothing to do with sacrifice or loss, but everything to do with being happier and having fun. I used the word "fun" purposely to capture the actual perspective which drew us to this adventure.

Picking Ravi up from the airport remains vividly imprinted in my mind. The entire adoption had been completed without our ever seeing him. We had decided, at a distance of thousands of miles, to be mother and father to this stranger, considered "damaged material" by other people's standards.

On the day of Ravi's arrival, Samahria and I waited impatiently at the airport terminal gate while hundreds of people came through the doors after clearing United States customs and immigration services. Suddenly, I recognized our contact person emerging from the crowd. He held the hand of this thin little boy whose dark brown eyes rapidly scanned the lines of waiting people. I leaped over the ropes, knelt directly in the path of this youngster and reached out my hands to him. He smiled at me. He knew! Then he lunged forward and jumped into my arms. I loved him in that very first instant. I would be his "Popi," as committed to him as to any of my other children.

So many people romanticize love. They talk of chemistry and bonding. Relationships take time to nurture and develop, they say. When I had known Ravi for only minutes, my love felt as strong and deep as the love I had for my oldest children, who had lived with me for over a decade. Love, like happiness, would never be a mystery to me again. I had witnessed the sweetness, the power and the miracle of a decision.

For the first six months, Ravi became an appendage, always holding on to my leg as if to find a secure place to anchor himself. Although he demonstrated an astute agility with his body, he seemed hesitant to speak, even in Spanish. In the years that have passed, this little guy has stretched himself and matured into a fine athlete and honor student. Just last year, he gave a speech in front of an auditorium filled with his classmates and was elected president of three grades.

More recently, we adopted a ten-year-old girl who had been a victim of poverty and abuse. This child of the streets, who had learned to steal and lie to survive, had been lifted out of strife-torn El Salvador to become part of our ever-growing family. Although her adoption had transpired with her complete permission and approval, she declared adamantly upon her arrival that she would not learn English or go to school . . . ever! We learned to recognize a softness behind her defiance and a deep yearning for closeness that her self-imposed isolation could not hide. We gave Sage several years of strong, yet gentle input before she could relax her guard and allow herself to love and trust others. Today, she loves learning, speaks English wonderfully, and has become one of the most helpful, affectionate and loving members of our family. Her presence has been and continues to be a blessing in our lives.

Each one of our six children has given us opportunities to access more of ourselves. Instead of being diminished or stretched too thin by their challenges, we have uncovered an ever-growing wellspring of love and ingenuity. As I teach a class, do a private session with someone or walk with my children through the surrounding forest, I feel I have found a sense of happiness, peace and communion with God that I once would not have dreamed possible.

II · Creating a Personal Vision to Live By

The eye sees what it brings to seeing.

SHELLEY

A fifty-six-year-old man, married with children and grandchildren, viewed himself as a realistic, no-nonsense person, definitely not the romantic or sentimental type. His verbal communication tended to be gruff and blunt, delivered always without any sugar coating. He withheld more than he shared. If he described a person or an event as "nice," he had given it his highest compliment. No one would ever accuse him of being exuberant. His childhood had been dominated by strict, sometimes abusive parents. When they hit him or punished him, they said they did it because they loved him. He came to hate the word "love" and never used it, not once, throughout his adult years. During a break in an afternoon

27

class, he shared with me a discovery he had made.

"I always thought love meant pain," he said. "Maybe that's not so, Bears. Today, I watched people in class use that word in many ways. Unhappily. Happily. Then I realized, hey, it's just a word. That's all. My parents gave it one meaning, but, me, well, I could give it another. I kept thinking, yeah, I could even get to like that word."

When class resumed, he asked to share his revelation with the other program participants. Then he turned to his wife, who had attended the seminar with him. He reached out and took her hand in an uncharacteristically graceful and tender gesture. He smiled as his bottom lip quivered and then, in a soft, sweet voice, said, "I love you." Tears filled his wife's eyes. In thirty-six years of marriage, she had never heard him say those words.

We can change. We can be different. We can defy history. Our past is but a memory dragged into the present moment. That moment is no more important or significant than the next. And in the next moment, we can change it all. We do it by changing our point of view . . . by changing our beliefs, as the man above did, and the woman below.

She had just celebrated her thirty-seventh birthday. She came, she said, to work on anger and forgiveness. Her mother had conceived her after being raped by an acquaintance. Wounded and meek, the woman never filed any charges. Now the child of that act of violence wanted to make peace with what she called "the unthinkable."

Her own successful marriage, her delight in her two sons, and the enjoyment of a developing sales career had been dimmed by the gnawing anger she directed at phantom images of a man she had never seen. Initially, she considered her intense emotions as a cross of outrage she would bear the rest of her life. Then, she held on to the bitterness to protect herself and those she loved from such "subhuman" behavior as the rape of her mother. Finally, exhausted by pain, she wanted to somehow move beyond her narrow view and come to a new understanding.

"This man has never seen me, though he knows I exist. He is old now, riddled with cancer. I have even located where he lives; I know his exact address. At first, when I found him, I thought about cursing him or beating him with my fists. Oh, God, I want out of this misery and all I do is get myself deeper in. Instead of practicing peacefulness, I practice rage!"

No one would fault this woman for her wrath. Some might even see justice in a finger-pointing confrontation with her "father." However, she knew she had been twice the victim: first, of a stranger's violence toward her mother and then of her own emotional violence toward herself. The first violence had passed years before; the second continued simmering inside.

While exploring these issues, she came to a crucial awareness. "If I continue to see him as terrible, I will never let go.
Never! I really have to look at this person differently for my
own salvation." She shook her head and sighed. "Okay. This
will probably sound stupid, but the man's a human being—
isn't he?" She smiled. "I know, Bears, you won't give me the
answers; I have to find them myself. Okay, then yes, I agree
with myself; he's a human being. Violent, probably miserable,
but still human like you and me."

"What does it mean to you to call him human?" I asked.

"It means he's fallible. And it means I don't have to hate
him forever. If I could just figure out how to let go of this
anger, well, then I'd be free and at peace with myself."

"How do you think you can let go of it?"

Her eyes closed as she covered her face with her hands.
In a muffled voice, she said, "I know how to do it, I really do.
Forgiving him would be letting go." With those words she
began to cry. In subsequent sessions and in dialogues with her
own husband, she formulated a plan of action which would
change her life.

Two weeks later, she flew to a remote midwestern city,
rented a car, and drove hundreds of miles to a small rural
village. She telephoned this man's younger daughter, the
product of an eventual marriage, and introduced herself without referring directly to the rape. The other woman hesitated,
then refused to invite her to the old man's home. She an-

nounced that she would come anyway; they could turn her away at his door if they wanted.

Old paint peeled off the side of the house. Shutters hung askew beside blackened windows. As she walked along a dirt path to the front door, she saw the woman who must have spoken with her on the phone standing on the porch with her arms crossed.

"I won't stop you," the woman declared coldly, then stepped aside while maintaining her obvious vigil.

After she knocked on the door several times, a man's voice told her to enter. One small lamp cast its dim light over the room. An old man, his shoulders hunched into his chest, sat quietly in a wooden chair. The deep lines on his face seemed chiseled by a crude and unforgiving knife. His reddened eyes peered at her uncomfortably. When he gestured for her to sit, his physical pain became apparent.

"I know who you are," he said in a whisper.

She couldn't talk. He was just a man, old and dying, nothing like the phantoms that had whirled in her mind. She struggled to find her voice. She had rehearsed the words hundreds of times on the plane. It's just a decision, she told herself.

Finally, in a whisper that matched his, she said: "I forgive you. I really do."

He nodded his head several times and then looked away. In a voice more audible, he said, "I'm sorry."

She rose to her feet. Just a human being, she thought, like me. Then she surprised herself by putting her arms around him. She had truly forgiven him. His words of apology had no meaning for her now; it was her new vision that had made her whole.

A vision (a frame of reference or viewpoint) is like an invisible friend we invent to help us make sense of unfolding circumstances. We create visions for the best of reasons: to protect ourselves, to honor those we love and to express caring. But we do not have to become prisoners of our perspectives; we can change them and our lives by developing a completely new world picture . . . one human step at a time.

A sixteen-year-old boy fell off a roof during a summer camp experience. Although he had not been seriously injured by the fall, he developed a strong aversion to ledges and high places. In fact, he even refused to enter the protected balcony of his grandfather's apartment. He avoided bicycle riding for fear of falling. When his parents pressed him to get help, he told them he needed time to conquer his problem and asked not to be pushed to do what he could not do.

One day, on his way home from school through a wooded lot, he heard the screams of two children. When he looked up, he saw them dangling precariously from the top walkway of a huge water tower. He considered going for help but realized they might fall before he returned. He thought for a moment more, then decided God had placed him in that exact spot for a reason and he could trust the reason. His fears evaporated. Without further hesitation, he ran to the ladder affixed to the side of the tower, climbed up over two stories and brought the children down safely.

We can scare ourselves or inspire ourselves. We can make the word "love" mean pain or use it as a celebration of caring. We can see people as objects of scorn or as human beings, though perhaps imperfect and capable of unhappy acts. We can generalize and cast clouds over all future experiences or invoke God to help us break through personal barriers. We are in charge. We are the architects of our own attitudes and experiences. We design the world by the way we choose to see it!

Our beliefs about the world and ourselves have profound ramifications, affecting all that we embrace around us and all that evolves within us. During the last decade, the National Institute for Neurological and Communicative Disorders and Stroke (NINCDS) conducted in-depth studies of people exhibiting multiple personalities. Some facts catalogued as part of the research leaped out at me and tickled my imagination. They demonstrated clearly the impact of our convictions and attitudes.

• One woman, who had the capacity to display three distinct personalities, had three menstrual periods each month, one for each personality.

• A man exhibiting multiple personas required completely different eyeglass prescriptions for each. In the morning, after assuming one personality, he was clinically nearsighted. At noon, after becoming the next person he wanted to be, he needed new glasses to compensate for far-sightedness. Each subsequent persona required yet another prescription.

• Another man, whose repertoire included nine distinct personalities, suffered a severe and, at times, life-threatening allergic reaction to citrus fruits. Any ingestion of citric acid would cause eight of his nine personalities to have hives, convulsions and seizures. His ninth personality, however, had a fetish for citrus fruits. While assuming this persona, he could consume enormous quantities of oranges and grapefruits without the slightest bodily disturbance.

If any one of us decided to see ourselves as many people within one bodily structure, then we could apparently create personalities so distinct that each would have its own physiology and could, perhaps, transform in seconds on a molecular as well as a cellular level. Such bits and pieces of information, as those from the NINCDS study, dance like excited children in my brain. I am awed by the wondrous possibilities they suggest!

The Way We Look at Life Determines Our Experience.

Such a simple insight presents each of us with an opportunity to make momentous changes in our lives. The only limits are the ones we create!

We can ask a new kind of question: not simply inquiring into "what is," but inquiring into what we want and what grasp of the universe would nurture and support a choice to be happier, more loving, more peaceful and more secure. Can we move away from the contemporary cauldron of pessimism to find a more useful and inspiring point of view? Rather than wait for a pie-in-the-sky apocalyptic event, we can take charge of our own evolution by changing our world view now.

The current cultural paradigm—the frame of reference from which we view the events unfolding locally and in our global village—suggests a scourge upon the land, with brother fighting brother, new diseases sweeping like plagues through generations of people, poverty and famine snarling at the doorsteps of human dignity, and a general ecological malaise hanging like a frightening veil over the planet's future.

Current events, as depicted by the news media, bombard our consciousness with one catastrophe after another, reinforcing a "victim" mentality. Reporters and newscasters endlessly parade, for our literary or visual consumption, the bodies of those killed, maimed or noticeably diminished by war, disease, violent crime, economic recession, poor parenting, drug or alcohol addiction, sexual abuse, food poisoning, train wrecks, air crashes, automobile collisions, tornadoes, hurricanes, floods and the like. Although we remain attentive, we numb ourselves, trying to put some distance between us and the brutality of those onslaughts. In the evening, we wonder how we made it through the day in one piece or, worse yet, how we will survive the unseen catastrophes of tomorrow.

We could decide, flat out, to stop watching and listening to the news . . . and to stop reading it, too. We have made an addiction out of being "informed," as if knowledge of disasters could somehow contribute to our sense of well-being and serenity. Our lives will never be enriched by the gloomy pronouncements of unhappy people, fearing and judging all that they see. They follow fire engines racing toward billowing black clouds of smoke and ignore the smiling youngster helping an elderly woman carry her grocery bags. One dramatic traffic accident on a major highway sends reporters scurrying, while the stories of four hundred thousand other vehicles that made it home safely go unnoticed. Newscasters replay over and over again a fatal plane crash captured on videotape but rarely depict the tenderness of a mother nurturing her newborn infant.

Simple acts of love, safe arrivals, peaceful exchanges between neighboring countries and people helping each other are noteworthy events. The media bias toward sensationalism and violence presents a selective, distorted and, in the final analysis, inaccurate portrait of the state of affairs on this planet. No balance here. We feed our minds such bleak imagery, then feel lost, depressed and impotent without ever acknowledging fully the devastating impact these presentations have on our world view and our state of mind.

Why not inspire ourselves rather than scare ourselves? We choose our focuses of attention from the vast menu of life's experiences. Wanting to be happy and more loving on a sustained basis directs us to seek peaceful roads less traveled. Though we might not determine all the events around us, we are omnipotent in determining our reaction to them. Some of us will live on the earth's crust searching for horror; others will lift the stones and see beauty beneath. Our embrace of life will be determined not by what is "out there," but by how we ingest what is "out there." Our view becomes almighty.

What we have been taught about ourselves and the universe around us conspires to have us believe that living requires awesome energy and great struggle. "No pain, no gain," we are told. "Life is a constant struggle." "You have to take the bad with the good." "You never really get what you want." "You're unlovable." "Something is wrong with you" (although it's never quite identified, you know it's there). "There is no justice." "No one cares." "Look over your shoulder and beware!"

These become communal mantras, shared with others and elevated to the status of treasured folklore. They color our vision and send us searching for the experience (rejection, attack, indifference) that we anticipate. Usually we find it! Our vision blossoms into a self-fulfilling prophesy, which each new experience tends to verify and reinforce. I never met a man who lived forever. I also never met a man who believed he could live forever. We become our beliefs. We get stuck in our heads.

Suppose we set aside the rigid concepts we might have learned about how the universe works. If we can now begin to entertain the possibility of many world pictures, then we might want to experiment by putting aside a logical, linear view of existence with fixed points and "hard facts" and consider a metaphor which reveals the ever-changing nature of the known universe.

We swim in a river of life. We can never put our foot into the river in the same place twice. In every second, in every millisecond, the water beneath us changes. Likewise, in every second, in every millisecond, the foot that we place into the river fills with new blood. Instead of celebrating the motion, we try to hold on to the roots and stumps at the bottom of the river, as if letting go and flowing with it would be dangerous. In effect, we try to freeze-frame life in still photographs. But the river is not fixed like the photograph and neither are we.

Ninety-eight percent of the atoms of our bodies are replaced in the course of a year. Our skeleton, which appears so fundamentally stable and solid, undergoes an almost complete transition every three months. Our skin regenerates within four weeks, our stomach lining within four days and the portion of our stomach lining which interfaces with food reconstructs itself every four or five minutes. Thousands, even millions, of neurons in our brain can fire in a second; each firing creates original and distinct chemistry as well as the possibility for new and different configurations of interconnecting signals. As billions of cells in our bodies keep changing, billions of stars and galaxies keep shifting in an ever-expanding space. Even the mountains and rocks under our feet shift in a never-ending dance through time. Life celebrates itself through motion and change.

Although we can certainly see continuity—seasons come and go, trees grow taller and people get older—we can acknowledge that each unfolding moment, nevertheless, presents a world different from that of the last moment. We could say that we and the world are born anew in every second and our description would be accurate scientifically. Therein lies an amazing opportunity for change. We can stop acting as if our opinions and perspectives have been carved in granite and begin to become more fluid, more open and more changeable, even inconsistent. We are in the river. We are the river!

Every stroke we make, every thought or action we produce, helps create the experience of this moment and the next. And the beliefs we fabricate along the way shape our thoughts and actions. Sounds rather arbitrary, some might say. It is! Quite simply, we try to move toward what we believe will be good for us and away from what we believe will be bad for us—operating always within the context of our beliefs. Even our hierarchies of greater "goods" and greater "bads" consist only of more beliefs. We hold our beliefs sincerely and defend our positions with standards of ethics or "cold, hard facts." We treat much of what we know and believe as irrefutable. We talk in absolutes. Once our beliefs are in place, we use all kinds of evidence to support them, quite unaware that we have created the evidence for the sole purpose of supporting whatever position we favor. In essence, we have become very skilled at "making it up."

Many years ago, my mother had surgery for breast cancer, followed by radiation treatments. Several years later the cancer reappeared in other parts of her body. Operations and additional radiation therapy disfigured and disabled her. Her dying process overwhelmed her and the rest of our family for years.

Not long after her death, we received a phone call from a researcher at the famed hospital where she had been treated, inquiring as to her current health. When informed of her passing, the researcher asked for the date of her death. I realized, on reflection, as he did, that she had died only a little more than five years after her initial surgery, although the cancer had continued to spread and more invasive treatment ensued. Since she had survived five years past the initial surgery and the study did not inquire into the quality of life during those years or the possibility of recurrences, the hospital representative indicated that my mother would become a favorable statistic for the hospital's cancer clinic.

Months later, major journals carried the news of this hospital's success in treating and effecting breast cancer cures based on a five-year survival rate. The agony of my mother's final journey had been filtered through the statistician's hand and transformed into data supporting the hospital's claims. The evidence had been gathered to support the beliefs of the gatherer and to further enhance the reputation of his facility and its methods. And so often we, the consumers of beliefs and evidence, buy just such "facts" as gospel.

Exploration of the belief-making game becomes even more beguiling as we pursue it further. Many years ago, after trying unsuccessfully to deal with a minor medical problem, I sought the input of an elderly Chinese physician and acupuncturist who had been educated in Beijing and Shanghai. In accordance with his beliefs, he began his examination by checking the twelve energy meridians in my body. He placed his fingers gently on my wrist and then, to my surprise, continued to stare at his watch. Finally, he shook his head.

"What's wrong?" I asked.

"Weak heart," he declared with great conviction.

My mouth dropped open. "Impossible," I countered.

"Weak heart," he repeated pointedly.

Surprised and concerned by his comment, I asked for further explanation. He noted that my heart beat only fifty-two times per minute, rather than the "normal" seventy-two to seventy-six times per minute.

"Oh," I sighed with relief, "I'm a runner. I jog six miles every day and have done so for over twelve years. My cardiovascular system has been well exercised," I added. "That's why, at rest, my heart beats so slowly." I had had a complete physical exam recently, including a stress test with an electrocardiogram, which determined that I had a well-toned and strong heart. I repeated what I had read, sprinkling my summary with additional information from my regular physician and the latest cardiovascular statistics.

"Now understand why weak heart," he said authoritatively. This eastern physician then explained that because of my continuous running, my heart had been fatigued; thus, it was no longer capable of putting out seventy-six beats per minute.

"Ever watch dog?" he said. "Breathe very fast. Heart beats fast. Twelve years, maybe fifteen years, dead. Big whales. Hmm, breathe slowly. Heart slow. Easy. Can live one hundred years. More, maybe." Then he explained that, in accordance with his "vision," the heart can beat only a finite number of times in a lifetime. By running, breathing fast and making my heart beat fast, he maintained, I had been using up those beats unnecessarily and had exhausted my heart muscle as well.

The exact same evidence in the hands of two different doctors led to profoundly opposing conclusions. I did note that the Chinese physician was a lively man in his late eighties (perhaps he had been saving up his heartbeats). What did I want to believe? In this case, my intention was to be healthy. Although keenly aware that two cultures held different "truths" about the same data, I still wanted to find a meaningful way for me to select beliefs and behavior which would support my health. I resolved the dilemma by choosing to consult what I call my "nonverbal/nonconceptual resource within." I would make a decision about running based on what felt good to me physiologically. I had pushed myself for years to make a certain quota of miles each week, sometimes ignoring fatigue and an internal inclination to ease my stan-

dard. I decided now I would run only as long as I felt energized to do so. I would gather new evidence to support my
new criteria or new belief. Within weeks, I trimmed my
mileage by almost fifty percent.

Our conclusions follow from our chosen biases (our chosen beliefs).

We Are Belief-Making and Belief-Consuming Creatures.

As children, we called it "make believe." People encouraged
us to be imaginative and creative, to fantasize and enjoy.
Then, as we aged, the guidance changed. Grow up! Be realistic! "Making believe" became the more serious game of
"making beliefs": judging, drawing conclusions, deciding
what's good and bad, right and wrong. All our emotions and
behaviors then follow from the beliefs we create.

Parents, priests, teachers, corporate executives and politicians compete busily to teach us or sell us beliefs so that they
can influence our feelings and behavior. They know, and we
soon learn, that winning the games of power, both personal
and political, depends on what we choose to believe. Nobel
Prize winners, homemakers, army generals, secretaries, physicians, truck drivers, lawyers, masons, journalists, carpenters,
advertising executives, have this in common: they operate
from their beliefs. How they vote; what sort of army they

support, if any; what purchases they make; where they live; whom they marry; what clothes they wear all flow from their beliefs.

A rather inventive and sophisticated example of belief peddling can be seen in the new and ever-evolving language of warfare. The military industrial complex seeks favorable public opinion in order to encourage congressional support for its products and activities. In recent years, it has been restructuring and reconstituting reality by using new buzzwords, intent on molding beliefs which would support its aims. The following phrases and word combinations come from various governmental reports and announcements dealing with military preparation and actions.

At first glance, a "re-entry vehicle" could appear inviting. We might anticipate a people or cargo carrier that always returns home. Not so! One example, among many, of a "re-entry vehicle" is a nine-megaton nuclear warhead. Army personnel now refer to "collateral damage" during military operations. This has no relation to disturbing lawns and shrubs at roadside. "Collateral damage" refers to the killing of civilians. Sending "Peacemakers" to other countries might gain wide support prior to the public's realizing "Peacemakers" are MX missiles. "Violence processor" has become the high-tech label for a fully equipped combat soldier.

Encountering the ingenious term "environmental adjustment," we might imagine a unique ecological thrust healthful to plants (and possibly chiropractic in nature!). However, this phrase means destroying an entire geographic area with a toxic chemical defoliant.

Of all the fanciful images that military belief-makers have tried to create, none seems more paradoxical and intriguing than the phrase used to describe peace. In their obvious effort to sell military vigilance, they refer to peace among nations as "permanent prehostility."

These propagandists (as all of us are for what we believe) try to harness our preferences and prejudices to their interests by employing a marketing strategy still in its infancy.

We can understand immediately the power of beliefs in the political arena and the marketplace, yet we do not readily apply that same clarity to ourselves. We function much like absorbing sponges, acquiring beliefs uncritically at a dizzying pace in order to take care of ourselves in the best way possible. The onslaught of beliefs has become so steady in our culture that often we ingest beliefs and repeat them to others without question or review. "This is the best country in the world." "We have a right to free speech." "Death is inevitable." "College prepares you for life." "Life is a series of ups and downs." "Feelings are like instincts; they just come upon you." "Nothing lasts forever." "Good health is often a matter of good genes and good luck."

To question beliefs like the ones listed above does not necessarily mean they are erroneous or invalid. However, in-quiry opens the door to understanding more fully *why* we believe what we do and whether or not we want to continue believing it. Do the beliefs we hold serve us? Do they empower us or lead us to feel impotent? Do they lead to happiness or unhappiness?

Frequently, we reformulate what other people say—the beliefs they sell—into conclusions or beliefs about ourselves. The avalanche of commentaries begins in childhood:

- "Be seen but not heard." (Conclusion: What I say doesn't matter.)
- "I know better than you." (Conclusion: I'm not intelligent enough to know.)
- "You are too young to understand." (Conclusion: When I get older, I'll get smarter—I hope.)
- "Don't question what I say; just listen." (Conclusion: Other people's statements are more important than my own.)
- "You make me unhappy." (Conclusion: I have the power to cause unhappiness in others.)
- "If you loved me, you'd keep your room neat." (Conclusion: If I don't do what my mother wants, it means I don't love her.)
- "Take the medicine or you won't get better." (Conclusion: Outside intervention is the only thing that will save me; I have nothing to do with my healing process.)

Once childhood and adolescence give way to the more mature years, then the messages appear to change, or do they?

· "If you loved me, you'd be more caring or sexually active." (Conclusion: I still have to do what people want in order to prove I love them.)

· "You'll never understand me." (Conclusion: It's not okay to disagree and have my own opinions.)

· "You make me furious!" (Conclusion: I cause what others feel.)

· "Can't you do it right?" (Conclusion: I'm ill-equipped; there must be something wrong with me.)

· "You can't expect to be healthy forever." (Conclusion: I have no control—disease and sickness are inevitable).

We learn our beliefs from others or deduce them from our own experiences. In effect, beliefs are interpretations and conclusions. What others say and teach us tells us about their thought processes and their beliefs. What we decide to "buy"—adopt and empower—tells us about our thought processes and our beliefs.

Despite all this belief manufacturing and belief consuming, we do not believe all that we are told. For instance, when told "The stock market is a good place to invest your money," some of us believe it, and some of us don't. We choose our beliefs freely; therefore, we can discard them if we decide. Nevertheless, we might note with fascination that our beliefs tend to be constant. We hold on to them for a long time, usually because we don't explore them or challenge them.

However, we can question our beliefs, not as a sign of disrespect or indictment of ourselves or others, but to give ourselves an opportunity to review, to reaffirm, to change and, most significantly, to facilitate happiness.

The impact of the beliefs we hold is profound. The ramifications can be devastating, but, conversely, they can be empowering and liberating. If I think something is wrong with me or that I am unlovable, I will probably have corresponding feelings associated with such beliefs—sadness, isolation and impotence. My actions will follow from that vision of myself. I might leave a relationship or bury myself in work to find meaning or a sense of self-worth. Ultimately, my body will reflect my mind-set with sluggishness, a suppressed immune system, vulnerability to disease and viruses and, perhaps, precipitate illness. We can indict ourselves and feel guilty or, in contrast, use the power of beliefs to determine more consciously what happens to us. With such a realization comes hope, strength and an opportunity to create ourselves anew.

Why, in the past, did we rush to judgment, rush to create interpretations or beliefs? The answer is quite simple: we create and hold beliefs to support what we think is best. A pertinent example is beliefs about unhappiness. We teach the value of discomfort as a means to growth, learning and enlightenment. "No pain, no gain." Our scriptures offer a vision of suffering as a method of purification. No wonder our culture teaches unhappiness, a very potent form of pain.

We use unhappiness to motivate ourselves and others. We use the fear of cancer to induce others to stop smoking, though ironically more cigarettes are now being sold than ever before. We hate our fat to prod ourselves to diet; yet more people are overweight now than at any other time in our history. We spank our children to teach them and express anger toward lovers to induce them to change, all of which leads usually to resistance rather than compliance. We arm millions of soldiers with devastating weapons of destruction in order to keep the peace, but then war becomes what we teach and the tool readily available to resolve conflicts.

Nevertheless, we push on! We teach misery as a sign of caring (if I am unhappy, you should be unhappy to show me you care) and as a sign of intelligence (conscientious people would be rightly unhappy about famine or disease; any opposing position would be unthinkable). It is no accident that we use the phrase "happy idiot" to suggest the inappropriateness and frivolity of sustained good feelings.

Finally, if all else fails, we threaten ourselves with the promise of future unhappiness (If John doesn't get home on time, I'll be angry. If I don't get that job, I will be heartbroken. If she doesn't love me, I'll be lost and desperate.).

Once they are articulated and itemized, our beliefs often sound somewhat bizarre and self-defeating. This is why review-

ing them provides us with a wondrous opportunity. Change the beliefs and we change the attitudes, thoughts, feelings and behaviors that come from them. Even after exploring our beliefs, if we choose to retain some of the ones we have, we would do so with strengthened conviction. Either position becomes a victory! The decision is ours, as it always has been.

A woman in her middle seventies came to our teaching center with the intention of dealing with her anger at a culture that had begun to dismiss her contributions and her wants because of her advancing age. She had noted in stores and in her bank that people spoke to her in loud little boy or little girl voices, as if they believed she could not hear or understand. Sometimes they addressed her as "dearie."

Although she had been a widow for twenty years, she now decided she was ready to have a meaningful relationship again, which she hoped would include sex. When she shared this desire with her friends, they changed the subject quickly. When she approached her grown children, they appeared startled and suggested that a desire for that type of physical contact at her age was less than appropriate. They, too, squashed the discussion. No one wanted to talk to her about her overriding concerns, she said, "No one, except, of course, you!" We both laughed. She delighted in being able to share her deepest thoughts without being judged or rejected. "I guess there's two times in life when you're not supposed to talk about sex," she mused, "when you're under ten and over seventy." She laughed again, thoroughly enjoying her insights.

In our sessions together, as she challenged and discarded the stereotypical beliefs held by her family and friends, an underlying issue surfaced. She realized that she had always been seeking approval from the important people in her life, cutting off her own desires in order to please others. As soon as she verbalized the scenario, she decided immediately that she no longer wanted to act in that way anymore. In addition, she concluded that having sex as part of a love relationship, even at her age, would not only be dignified, but absolutely thrilling! Armed with her new perspective and a new attitude, she returned home.

Four months later, I received a letter from this spirited lady. As I opened the envelope, a photograph fell onto my desk. The picture captured a beaming portrait of this woman arm-in-arm with a smiling male companion. The message on the reverse side said, "This is me with my boyfriend. We just moved in together. He's fifty-eight years old, a great friend and a wonderful lover. Not bad for an old lady!"

People can change at any age. Where there is life, there

is possibility. Even ancient beliefs can be overturned or re-placed in a matter of moments. We are the river!

My wife and I felt honored to be invited to attend the home birth of one of our staff members. We tried in many different ways to assist the two attending midwives as well as the parents-to-be. A festive, yet relaxed atmosphere permeated their apartment. To be additionally useful, I photographed the evolving adventure for them, trying to capture the special moments of support and caring these two adventuresome souls shared. As Laura's contractions became more and more frequent, one midwife listened diligently to the baby's heartbeat and nodded with an approving smile. Laura's cervix began to dilate appropriately. The time of birth neared. But then, suddenly, the contractions stopped completely. The midwives tried several different noninvasive techniques to restart the process but to no avail.

Laura lifted her huge form off the bed and began pacing. One midwife, obviously concerned, suggested that if her contractions did not begin again soon it might be prudent to go to the hospital. Laura shook her head. A home birth had always been her dream. She wanted to stay; however, her general discomfort kept increasing. Neither standing, walking nor lying down eased it. Finally, she retreated to the bathroom, sat down stark naked on the toilet seat and experienced some relief. The midwives kept expressing their concern. Laura asked if I would join the three of them. I sat down between the sink and the bathtub. Laura looked absolutely elegant as she cradled her huge abdomen in her hands and smiled weakly at me.

"I'm getting scared," she whispered to me. She reached out her hand, and I held it for a few moments. "Bears, maybe you could ask me some questions, especially about the contractions."

"Sure," I said smiling. "Why do you think they stopped?"

One of the midwives began to answer by stating clinically the possible physiology involved. She also volunteered that this might be an inappropriate time to ask questions. Laura leaned toward her and said, "I want to figure this out! The questions are fine." Then, she turned to me again. "I think I know what happened," she continued, "but I'm embarrassed to say."

"Why?" I asked. The answer which followed, though particular to her own process, reminded me of my own past questions and ones that I have heard often expressed by prospective parents.

"Well, we all work with many different people at the Institute," she said, "but me, I'm being trained to work with special children. To love them. Not to judge them. And suddenly, when I was lying there and it was getting closer, I got really scared." She paused as if to catch her breath. "Suppose I have a special child like some of the children we see or like you and Samahria did. Suppose my child can't talk or see or move his legs. You know, for everyone out there, it's just a vague possibility. For me, it's very, very real. We work with kids all the time who are less than what the world calls 'perfect.' " Tears began to stream down her cheeks.

"Why are you crying?" I asked softly.

"Oh, I guess I expect more from me. I really love what I do, I love the kids, but I'm not sure it would be okay if my child had a problem," Laura admitted.

"Why wouldn't it be?"

She started itemizing every birth defect, every developmental delay and every neurological dysfunction she could imagine. We looked at the realities of each one together: Down Syndrome, autism, cerebral palsy, spina bifida, mental retardation, aphasia, epilepsy, nonspecific brain dysfunction and the like. One by one, she discarded her fears about these possibilities. We persisted for about twenty minutes; then she held her hand up.

"I got it," she said. "I just decided. I can be strong, very strong. I will love and treasure my baby no matter what happens! I'm not afraid anymore."

A soft, radiant smile spread across her face as her abdomen pitched upward into a pointed crown in response to a powerful contraction. Her husband came to her side and coached her breathing through the movement. As we led her back into the bedroom, Laura squeezed my hand.

Less than thirty minutes later, she delivered a healthy, sweet little boy.

We can observe our bodies and learn much about our beliefs. Physical symptoms can help make our wants and concerns more apparent. Thoughts occur body-wide; intelligence exists everywhere in our system. When we think, we create new and distinct electromagnetic impulses and chemical substances throughout our entire physical form. When we say we have changed our mind, we have made a statement of fact. Our minds as well as our bodies change physically each time we change a belief.

No one judged Denise more severely than she did herself. As she sat silently and half listened to the other members of her group share on the opening night of a personal growth seminar at The Option Institute, she rehearsed over and over what she would say. When her turn came, she mumbled inaudibly and never once looked up at anyone else in the room. A casual observer might have perceived her to be timid and shy, but she characterized herself as inept and dull. Therapy had not helped. Explorations of her past with a psychologist had never yielded any "ah-ha" revelations.

During a sequence in which participants paired themselves with just one other person, Denise conversed much more easily. I noticed an animation I had not seen in previous sessions. As soon as we returned to a single large group, she faded, never vocalizing an opinion or sharing anything intimate about herself. She loved people but felt incapable of participating effectively in a group. She used her discomfort as proof of her ineptitude and her belief in her ineptitude generated her discomfort. She had trapped herself in a circle of misery.

On the fourth morning of our time together, I led the group through a vigorous series of disconnected experiences, then I asked them to freeze in their places. As they held their positions, I suggested they be open to experimenting in the safety of this human laboratory. Could they drop any limiting beliefs they had of themselves and create a new personal vision that would enable them to be the facilitator and lead the group through an improvised experience of communion and fellowship? When they indicated their willingness, I called out Denise's name and announced, "The class is yours."

She stared at me aghast, giving me nothing less than direct and intense eye contact—a first for Denise. As I withdrew to the back of the room, everyone waited. Denise later told the group that her first impulse was to run, jump down the stairs and leave the building. But then, in what she experienced as expanded time, she touched a profoundly peaceful place within herself and dared to create a vision of herself as a commanding yet gentle teacher. She imagined the power her voice would have and what it would be like to look directly at people as she had looked at me. Then Denise did the seemingly impossible; she jumped into her dream, casting aside her judgments and doubts.

In a voice strong yet soothing, she gathered the participants into a circle and then led them through an open-eyed meditation that was at once original and inspiring. At the end of the segment, the group applauded and gave Denise a standing ovation. She held her hands in front of her mouth and giggled.

Later that morning, five others took their turn at leadership. Ultimately, the class voted Denise to be the most effective among them. She remained high-profile for the rest of the program, never reclaiming her old beliefs about being inept or dull. She continued to be outrageously open and communicative even after her return home. Two years later, I received an invitation to one of her growing number of public speaking engagements.

If we change one belief, we change the feelings and behaviors that come from that belief. If we change our vision, which consists of a tapestry of beliefs, we alter an amazing conglomerate of feelings and behaviors at once. Neither endeavor takes any more energy than the other.

Our Beliefs Create Our World Picture, Which We Then Transmit to Others.

As individuals, each of us becomes a force within a shared field of ideas and visions. Two powerful aspects of our interactions can be discerned easily. First, we can acknowledge ourselves as receivers. We see, we hear, we smell, we taste, we touch and we consume and digest beliefs. Much like a television set, we receive a variety of signals. But now we can recognize our authority over the tuner or channel changer and ask ourselves what messages we want to invite into our homes and our minds. We are not talking about censorship or putting blinders on; we are speaking of exercising more consciously our right to determine the types of inspirations we want to bring into our lives.

In addition to receiving, we transmit our ideas and visions. As transmitters, we can be seen as similar to a television or broadcasting station. Our lives become beacons, communicating the attitudes we assume, the beliefs we create and the actions we take. We become more than role models; we seed the field of human experience with our perspectives and deeds.

A thirty-year-old mother, who had arranged private, individual sessions for herself and for her child at our learning center, asked in agony why her adolescent son would actually lift his hand to her and threaten bodily assault. When questioned gently and without judgments, the boy explained his action quite openly. Since his mother hit him and his sister to express her disapproval, he similarly used the threat of force to express his resistance to her.

Parents ask many questions about the perplexing behavior of their children. "Why does she complain all the time?" "Why does he shout angrily when he doesn't get his way?" "How come my child seems so ungrateful?" Although children learn from the media, friends and their own experiences, often the lessons learned at home have the most impact. We can use the behaviors of those around us to stimulate questions about our own transmissions. Do we complain? Do we shout? Do we fail to express gratitude? Our answers tell us not only what we teach those around us but also what we put into the human collective and reinforce for others as well as ourselves.

Our beliefs and attitudes not only bubble to the surface in our feelings and behaviors but also are apparently transmitted on subtle levels as well. Once, when working with a nonverbal special child, we introduced a volunteer into the room as an observer. The child withdrew almost immediately from participating with her regular teacher and scurried across the room, clearly putting distance between herself and this new arrival. When the volunteer left, the child rejoined her teacher and participated easily and joyfully once again. Later, when I questioned the young man about his experience as an observer, he admitted feeling exceedingly uncomfortable and judgmental of the little girl's wild head movements and hand flapping.

We have noticed over and over again that nonverbal children rely on their ability to pick up attitude "transmissions" even when the initiator camouflages his or her discomforts with smiles. They know. They have a capacity, akin to radar, to pick up nonvisible signals. Words, even actions, do not distract them from getting a quick "fix" on a person's level of comfort. We all have that same capacity, but, unlike the special child, we have not maximized our skill. Many times, as verbal people, we focus on words alone. Yet on other occasions, we do "read" between the lines and take in data communicated less overtly.

The power of our beliefs and visions shape the character of our personal realities and impact on others around us. Recent scientific studies suggest that the "reach" of belief transmissions might go beyond anything we have ever imagined.

A contemporary biologist has noted a community of

shared information among species, which he calls morphogenetic fields. Essentially, his unfolding theory suggests that species, even groups of species, share an invisible and intangible communications field which can be observed and tested.

Early experimental efforts to teach rats to move through mazes yielded some startling results. The first group of rats performed endless trial-and-error rituals before finding their way through the maze. They succeeded at the task only with great difficulty. The second group of rats appeared somewhat more proficient. Subsequent experiments with genetically unrelated groups of rats, who had never before seen such mazes, moved through the mazes as if they had been pretrained. Somehow training some members of the species impacted on the abilities of all the others.

In other research, a group of behaviorists took pigeons, believed to be quite uneducable, and tried a behavioral approach to teach them to peck on lighted panels in what became known as the Skinner box. Initially, it took a long teaching period to train the pigeons to just begin the pecking. Researchers find that pigeons now peck at lighted panels easily and quickly. Some people claim now that anyone could go to any city in the world, coax a pigeon into a Skinner box, and, in short order, perhaps only minutes, teach the creature to peck on lighted panels—a humorous suggestion about an outrageous yet testable reality. Teach one or more of a species and all the members begin to learn the lesson.

The implications escalate when we ask if our transmissions are confined to species within the animal kingdom. In 1966, one of the foremost experts on polygraph machines (lie detectors) tried a unique experiment. One morning, in his office, rather than hooking his lie detector to a person, he attached the electrodes to the palmlike leaves of a plant. His initial printout from the plant matched similar ones he had recorded when testing people at rest. He knew an individual under stress, frightened or agitated, would cause changes in the meter readings of the polygraph. Could he produce a similar response from plants?

He proceeded to water the plant to see if there was a measurable impact on the polygraph. There was no significant difference. Perhaps the analogy he hoped to demonstrate had no basis, he thought. However, he decided to escalate the experiment and precipitate stress by introducing a hot cup of coffee and dipping the leaves of the plant into the scalding liquid. Again, the reading did not register any significant change. He fantasized about what act he could perform to trigger a response in the plant if that was, indeed, possible. He considered finding matches and actually burning the leaves. As he rose from the chair to execute his idea, he noticed the readout on the polygraph moving frenetically. In subsequent experiments, he demonstrated repeatedly that his violent visualizations affected the foliage and plant life around him.

We could conclude from these studies that all living things communicate with each other through intelligence or morphogenetic fields. The implications are staggering. What each of us learns has the potential of becoming a message to all humankind and, perhaps, to all other life forms as well. Each life has profound significance.

A new question now arises. If we want to be happy and support a universe that nurtures such an endeavor, what data would we want to feed into the human collective? What would we want to engender and reinforce? What gifts of awareness, what deeds, would we want to give our children, our friends, our lovers, our parents, our community, humankind, the animals, the plants, even the rocks?

Whatever we put into the river will mix in the current and bounce back to us. If just one of us changes our beliefs and teaches happiness and love, then that attitude or information goes into the connective tissue of the community and enhances the aptitude for happiness of the entire human group.

People spend years, even lifetimes, rummaging through old memories and philosophies accumulated throughout the centuries in the pursuit of happiness or the promised land (where people are happy, loving and peaceful). The answer lies not behind us. We have to look forward toward a new vision that we can create—not merely in our lifetime, but right now!

III · The Happiness Option

*Most folks are about as happy
as they make up their minds to be.*

ABRAHAM LINCOLN

If we're so smart, why aren't we happy? Because we have not yet created the vision to support such a wonderful reality. But we can! We are the belief makers!

Each vision brings its own life experience and technology. Oftentimes, the impact defies our imagination. The search "out there" captivates us and inspires us to take many adventures. In the dazzle of contemporary living, we find comforts and accoutrements to tickle our every whim. We can fly. We can freeze images on film. We can use invisible radio waves to bring music, movies and mysteries into our living rooms. We can perform delicate laser surgery to restore sight and fabricate massive steel beams to construct buildings that soar a thousand feet into the sky. We can restart stopped hearts. We can cook with microwaves and use the components of atoms to create vast reservoirs of energy for commercial as well as military use. Our expanding inventiveness knows no bounds.

Yet the internal vision that drives us seems peculiarly antiquated. We express anger in similar proportions as we did thousands of years ago when we fought with stones. We judge people as we did hundreds of years ago when we belittled and imprisoned others whose beliefs or lives differed from ours. We live with daily discomfort as we play out our fears with disease, drugs, alcohol, suicide, rape and murder. Everything has changed; yet nothing is different. We have only become better at making war and more sophisticated at dulling our senses to what we don't want to see.

In the face of such immense data and intelligence, what could we create (conjure up in our lives) by changing our internal vision and the attitude with which we embrace ourselves and those around us? Could we take some familiar words, like happiness, love and peace and use our ingenuity to make them graspable and tangible now? And if we did, would we be entering an age of transformation more profound than any other witnessed on this planet?

Is Happiness an Impossible Dream?

All dreams appear impossible before someone makes them tangible. Desire combined with passion and the ingenuity of the mind has given birth to airplanes, space shuttles, submarines, organ transplants, mechanical hips and hearts, religious freedom, governments elected by the people and even short-term peace among nations. Desire combined with passion and the ingenuity of the mind can now give birth to happiness as a sustained and transforming human experience.

What does it mean to be happy? Some call happiness a feeling of satisfaction, comfort, fulfillment and inner peace. Others refer to joy, excitement and communion. The sensation of happiness might be unique to each of us; however, we know when we're there. We can note certain common characteristics. When we are happy with ourselves, we are accepting of ourselves (not judging ourselves). When we are happy with others, we are accepting of them (not judging others). Happiness brings us closer together rather than pushing us apart. But above all, happiness makes love tangible. To love someone fully and completely is to be happy with that person, to accept him without judgments and celebrate his existence. To love ourselves is to be happy with who and what we are, to accept ourselves without judgments and celebrate our own existence.

Over and over again, in sessions with clients, I have heard

children say to their parents, lovers say to their spouses and friends say to close companions, "Please, can't you just love me and accept me as I am?" In effect, they are asking the other person to be happy with them. They might still wish to respond to requests to change, but they ask that love not be conditional on their changing.

Most of us recoil from the criticism of others, yet we go home and condemn ourselves for being too fat, too slow, too dumb or too impatient. What we may vocally or silently want from others, we deny ourselves. But we can become the gift-givers to others and ourselves, and the gift we can offer is our happiness and the peace, love and acceptance that flow from it.

Without the clouds of discomfort (fear, anger, depression, anxiety, hate, jealousy, sadness), we free ourselves to see more clearly, to understand more deeply and to be more open and energized in all the pursuits of our lives. In contrast, unhappiness takes an awesome daily toll. Unhappiness diverts us, diminishes our stamina, drains our energy and leaves us performing an endless variety of self-defeating acts. War, terrorism, rape, drug addiction, child abuse and stomach ulcers are but a few of the testimonials to misery.

No single energy can be more impactful on this planet than the joy and well-being emanating from one truly happy and loving person. When we are committed to creating a peaceful new world, inside and outside, the old data become irrelevant. But we have to begin someplace . . . with someone. Why not with you and me and whomever else decides to pursue happiness with strength and passion?

Although I could say that I made my journey toward happiness a lengthy process and screamed and kicked my way there, I now know that I didn't have to walk that road. Due to my own lack of clarity, I missed the signposts. We can empower our pursuit of happiness and access shortcuts by making simple decisions and implementing them as a daily practice. Such decisions empower us with an attitudinal advantage in every situation . . . every day of our lives. Not a magical process! Not mystical! When we take happiness and love off the pedestal, we make them achievable options. The steps can be easy. Perhaps the most significant missing ingredient for me during those early years had been my unwillingness to establish a clear intention to make happiness a priority, to make happiness *the* priority.

We can begin by recognizing that we have already had practice in creating personal happiness. We do it all the time in small, yet meaningful ways. I call it "happiness by makeup, music and Häagen-Dazs."

A friend, who had been a guest in our home, collided into me early one morning as she rushed down the hallway. Grumpily, she said, "Don't look at me and don't talk to me;

I'm not civil company for anybody. I don't have my face on."
Then she disappeared into the bathroom. I smiled. In my
estimation, she clearly had her face on. However, she wanted
to "dress" her face and pamper herself in front of the mirror.
Why? To make herself happy. One hour later, appearing
amazingly bright-eyed, she hugged me at the breakfast table
and announced how glorious she felt. She had used her makeup as a vehicle to generate happiness.

Another friend used to come home after a busy day at the
office, crumple his coat on a chair in the hallway, then moan
and groan his way into the living room. He would mutter
something about traffic, unreasonable people and "burnout."
Moving with obvious fatigue, he would fumble grumpily with
the remote control switch to his stereo and finally manage to
turn on his favorite radio station. Within seconds, he would
kick off his shoes, lean back in a soft chair and just listen. His
grimace would disappear almost instantly and a soft smile
would dawn on his face. He had orchestrated an amazing
transformation; he had created personal happiness and used
the vehicle of music to do it.

Over the years, I have seen myself expend a great deal of
energy to administrate our teaching center, teach a class,
prepare a lecture or finish an article. At the end of the day
or evening, I might rub shoulders with other staff and friends
who have similarly expended much energy in their varied
endeavors. Inevitably, someone will suggest "innocently" that

we share some pints of Häagen-Dazs. Ten minutes later, two, four or six of us will sit happily around a table stuffing our faces. We used ice cream, not only as a reward, but also as a stimulus to be happy or happier and it worked just beautifully.

The myth underlying such well-intended activities would be that makeup, music and Häagen-Dazs bring happiness. Not so! We give ourselves that feeling of happiness either while anticipating, indulging in or recalling the experience. However, what we generate and feel has nothing directly to do with the stimulus outside and everything to do with the happiness option we trigger inside. What we discovered is that we can access that mechanism within as a choice or completely self-generated decision without requiring such external support as makeup, music and Häagen-Dazs. We can be happy without a reason . . . happiness is reason enough in itself.

A dear friend and colleague, Steven, who feels the same excitement about happiness that I do, had a fascinating experience with his four-year-old daughter's friend, a little boy who had come to their home one weekend afternoon for an extended visit. This child and his mother made a theatrical entrance by engaging in a physical and verbal tug-of-war over how long the boy could stay. The woman shook her head self-consciously as she pleaded with her son Danny, then screamed at him angrily. He escalated his unhappiness by moving from whining to crying. Finally, she separated from her child and said apologetically that she would return to pick him up in three hours as previously agreed.

The boy's dry crying, although somewhat abated, persisted even after his mother left. Steven tried to engage the youngster, but the little guy kept sobbing. Steven then turned to his daughter and smiled questioningly. She pulled her father's ear toward her face and whispered a short commentary, observing that Danny must be very unhappy but also predicting that he would be very nice when he stopped crying. Minutes later, in response to her offer to share yogurt with him, her young friend shoved her away, whining his dismay. Steven interceded, requesting that the boy follow him onto the side porch and sit with him on a bench.

"I don't think you know this, Danny," Steven said playfully, "but you have come to visit the happy house . . . yes indeed. By the way you are acting, I guess you believed this was just any old house. Well, it's not. This house is for happy people. If you want to come into this house, all you have to do is be happy. That's it! Very simple. You can also choose to stay unhappy if you'd like; I'd want you to know that, too. So why don't you think it over and let me know?"

He patted the boy gently on his shoulder and went back into the house. Within thirty seconds he heard a loud knocking on the open screen door. Steven responded immediately.

"Yes," he said enthusiastically to the little boy.

"I'm ready to come in now." A big smile lit up Danny's face. "I'm happy and I'm ready to come into the happy house."

With great fanfare, Steven ushered the child into his home for a second time. For the next three hours, this youngster played easily, comfortably and cheerfully with Steven's daughter. Not once did he cry, whine or grimace. Later, his mother arrived, thanked Steven and then guided her son to a waiting car. As they walked toward the vehicle, Danny started to whine almost immediately. By the time he reached the car, he was crying.

When we inspire others to be happy, we inspire ourselves. Every situation, including the one with Danny, becomes an opportunity. Each step we take counts. Children allow us to see the happiness option and the unhappiness option in action. They demonstrate an amazing power to turn their switches on and off at will. As adults, we are no less powerful.

Samahria and I, accompanied by some of our children, waited patiently in the check-out line. Crowds had descended on the supermarket for last-minute food shopping in anticipation of the Christmas holiday season. The staccato beep of lasers reading prices off packages mixed harmoniously with familiar holiday music being played on the sound system. Ski jackets, fur caps, mittens and woolen scarves wrapped the bodies of those waiting in line behind their carts filled with food. Although many shoppers appeared blank faced, more than the usual number smiled at one another. The moderately festive mood remained intact until a two-year-old girl, sitting in the seat of her mother's shopping cart, began screaming loudly.

People turned to see what problem had arisen. The child apparently wanted to consume the potato chips and other snacks inside the cart, but her mother had refused. In response, she protested with loud noises, tears, a flushed face and kicking. Her mother, somewhat embarrassed, maintained her position while trying to calm her daughter with quiet words. The child escalated her antics. By now, people in almost every line watched. Some grimaced their obvious disapproval. Others gave the child sympathetic glances. One woman leaned over the shelves in her aisle and demanded the mother do something—anything—immediately.

Suddenly, the store's Santa Claus appeared. He searched through the crowds of people for the tantruming child. Once he located her position, he pushed his padded body through several lines, shouting his "Ho! Ho! Ho!" As soon as he reached her, he placed a colorful candy cane into her hand. The little girl stopped screaming immediately and smiled broadly through her tears. As she opened the candy wrapper, surrounding adults watched approvingly. An older woman kept nodding her head and saying, "Good." Some people applauded. One man proclaimed, "Santa saved the day."

My thirteen-year-old daughter watched the entire event with great fascination. She looked up at me and laughed. "Santa didn't save the day; he just taught that little girl that unhappiness pays. If you scream and cry, you get candy. Now I'll bet when she goes to the next store, she'll do the same thing and get more goodies."

We weren't born unhappy; we learned to be unhappy. And, in addition, we have become masters at teaching and reinforcing unhappiness. In small, seemingly insignificant ways, we "save the day" but lose another life to misery. When we reward anger, we teach violence and war. When we support happiness, we teach love, peace and acceptance. We have the choice.

The early days of my pilgrimage in pursuit of happiness appear rather comical in retrospect, though at the time I believed every choice to be crucial and every step more important than the last. Ironically, rather than finding comfort and clarity, I encountered, and chose to embrace, the conventional wisdom advocating the inevitability of misery.

While working during the day and taking graduate courses in philosophy and psychology at night, I decided to intensify my learning further by going into psychoanalysis. I wanted to understand everything about the human psyche. More important, I wanted to overcome my anger and frustration with a world that seemed inhospitable and incomprehensible. During some early sessions, I moaned and groaned, incriminating myself and protesting the actions of others. As I walked toward the door in the concluding moments, the therapist often put his arm on my shoulder parentally and said, "You're really working on it. Good session. Just stay with it." However, on other rare occasions, I talked effusively about recent accomplishments and about seeing my life as moving productively ahead. When those sessions terminated, the analyst walked me to the door and said, "Maybe next time you'll get down to it and really work."

His message was clear. Be anxious, uncomfortable, fearful and frustrated and the session would be deemed productive and useful; be cheerful and optimistic and I would be seen as avoiding issues, the session not helpful or meaningful. Wanting to be a good student, I internalized the learning quickly. Every time I rode up to the psychoanalyst's office, I spent my time in the taxi thinking about every miserable and uncomfortable event I could conjure up. When I arrived finally for my session, I would be duly unhappy, ready to plunge headfirst into the abyss. I actually did this routine for years. Unwittingly, I became a student of misery rather than happiness.

Finally, when I decided to graduate from this process in my middle twenties, I noted that I still had fears, discomforts and anxiety. In a rare discussion with me, the analyst stated with great conviction that being human means having fears, discomforts and anxiety. What he had done with me, he noted, was teach me how to cope more successfully with those feelings. But they would never disappear, he assured me. He truly believed what he said and I had adopted and empowered those beliefs myself. However, as I listened to him speak during our last session, I became aware of wanting so much more. I did not want to be realistic, as he suggested. I wanted to be happy.

Illusion #1 Unhappiness now gets us happiness later. Not so! Using misery to fight misery just adds to the misery . . . pure and simple.

Illusion #2 Unhappiness is a natural, unavoidable characteristic of the human condition. Not so again! Unhappiness follows from certain beliefs and judgments, which we choose and which we can change.

So often, we hear ourselves and others make statements like the following: "She made me angry!" "He got me upset!"

"If my parents had been kinder or more supportive, I would have been happier." "Balancing my checkbook drives me crazy." "Your questions about our relationship make me feel insecure." "Their proposition got me excited." We talk as if our emotions (anger, upset, happiness, craziness, insecurity or excitement) are caused by people and/or events outside of us.

While still attending high school, our older daughters, Bryn and Thea, had an adventure which challenged them to question the origin of their feelings. One afternoon, they brought their youngest brother to a pizza parlor where they sat with fellow students at a large round table. Sweet Tayo, of Hispanic, South American Indian and miscellaneous ancestry, had turned very black in the summer sun. His large, inquisitive eyes accented his flat, wide nose and thick, rubbery lips. One teenager, who kept peering at him, said finally, "I guess you're babysitting for *that* little boy."

"No, no," Bryn declared, as she eyed Tayo proudly, oblivious to the emphasis in the statement. "We love to have him with us . . . he's our brother." Then she proceeded to talk to these acquaintances from school about the circumstances of his adoption. The girl who made the initial comment laughed smugly. "Why'd you do that?" Bryn asked.

"Oh, nothing," the girl teased sarcastically. "So your brother's a spic!" The ethnic slur reverberated throughout the restaurant.

Bryn lunged across the table, grabbed the girl by her

jacket and shouted, "Don't you ever dare talk about my brother or anyone like that again!" As the two budding young women rose to their feet, Bryn realized, as she recalled later, that her potential opponent was substantially larger and stronger than she. Immediately she reconsidered her anger and her aggressive posture.

In contrast, Thea laughed upon hearing the comment made about her brother. She found it strange and silly that someone could be so prejudiced. She dismissed the reference and refused to give the word any power. In addition, Thea suggested to the other girl that she might want to ask herself why she used such words and what she believed they meant.

When our three children returned home, our entire family gathered for a discussion about the incident. We talked about unhappiness, prejudice and words. But most pointedly, we all examined Bryn's and Thea's radically different responses to the exact same data. Both of them loved their little brother and felt protective of him. Bryn decided the comment meant something about Tayo and therefore became upset and attempted to defend his honor. Thea considered the girl's statement a reflection of the speaker, not Tayo, and felt amused by her distorted thinking.

Each daughter had had a choice. The ethnic slur did not make one unhappy and the other comfortable. Each girl decided to view the experience from her own unique and personal perspective (her world view), and, therefore, the two created different emotional experiences for themselves. If an event has the power to cause a specific response, then both girls would have reacted the same. Events are events. Each of us chooses our responses by how we decide to view them and by what beliefs and judgments we engage during the process. No one can be inside our heads pulling our strings. We do that for ourselves.

We could take such self-empowerment and see it as damnation. Ugh! We can make ourselves unhappy! We can make ourselves miserable! However, we could, on the other hand, see the possibility of such a choice as most liberating. If we have the power to make ourselves uncomfortable and angry, then we must also have the power to give ourselves the experience of comfort and peace of mind. Rather than be emotional victims of circumstances or blame other people for what we do and feel, we can take charge! We choose our state of mind. *We are the belief makers. In this universe, happiness is a choice and misery is optional (not inevitable).*

Is the Pursuit of Happiness Valid or Merely Self-Serving?

A college professor who attended one of my lectures labeled the pursuit of happiness trivial, self-indulgent and self-serving. I don't know what his experiences may have been, but I have noted that when people are happy, they are much more loving, supportive and available to themselves and those they touch. However, most "reasonable" people might argue that dealing with poverty, sickness, war and nuclear disarmament should certainly take precedence over a person's concern for individual happiness. The implication is that happiness, as the professor claimed, is not only self-serving but limited in impact and therefore not worthy of elevated status.

And yet, the founding fathers of our own government viewed the subject as so significant that they included the "pursuit of happiness" as an inalienable right in the Declaration of Independence. Beyond memorizing that document and those words as students, few of us, if any, studied the subject of happiness as attentively as we did language arts, mathematics, social studies and science. We never learned to acknowledge such a focus as truly valid or valuable. Although schools offer a vast array of subject areas for study (literature, history, psychology, biology, business administration, medical science, ecology, astrophysics, nautical engineering), no primary school, high school or university offers courses in the pursuit of happiness. No wonder we have learned to disregard the subject or "put it aside" for what we conclude to be more immediate and significant concerns.

The irony is that for ourselves individually and for the planet collectively there perhaps is no more pressing issue than personal happiness. To be happy (and all that "happy" implies—comfortable, loving, accepting, nonjudgmental, joy-ful, at peace with oneself) might in fact be the most pertinent prescription for dealing with what most of us are concerned with on a global, familial and personal basis.

So often we strive to change the world around us by changing others. We focus on external solutions to problems which can appear so overwhelming and complex that any reasonable hope of success seems remote. "What can I do?" we ask ourselves in despair. "I'm just one person."

Have we overlooked the most obvious and achievable approach to our problems even though at first it might appear simplistic—to be happy and loving?

If just one person changes, becomes happier, touches another with a more loving and peaceful hand, then the world has, indeed, become a more peaceful place. If each of us acknowledges him- or herself as one entity in an interlocking network of interactions (as lover, parent, friend, child, sibling, coworker, citizen), then, like the stone dropped in a pond, our evolution will cause countless ripples. Our capacity to change enables us to make a truly profound difference in the world.

In case studies that I documented in my books *Giant Steps* and *A Land Beyond Tears* I came to see over and over again that when one person overcomes anxiety, insecurity, drug dependency, physical disability, fear of death, the trauma of rape, the agony of divorce or any other black hole of personal discomfort, all those around that person are touched and inspired by his or her triumphs. As one person becomes happier, his or her attitudinal change alters the dynamics of every interaction with others, thereby impacting on a vast fabric of interwoven human relationships. Rather than dismiss this wellspring of power in you, in me or in any other single individual, can we harness it to make a difference?

The following examples might sound bizarre initially, but we could, nevertheless, consider in all seriousness the possible impact on a nation by a happy and loving head-of-state, on an army by a happy and loving general, on children by a happy and loving parent, on a relationship by a happy and loving spouse, on a patient by a happy and loving nurse, on a student by a happy and loving teacher, on a caller by a happy and loving telephone operator, on a traveler by a happy and loving bus driver. If happiness means that we become easier, more comfortable with ourselves, more accepting, respectful, excited and appreciative of what we do and with whom we interface, would we not then become a gift to all those we meet? Would we not become a continuously incredible gift to ourselves as well?

Would Sustained Happiness Be Detrimental?

We create myths to explain what we do not understand. The Greeks created Zeus and the land of Elysian Fields to explain

God and heaven. Science fiction novelists depict exotic alien creatures to represent other possible life forms which might or might not exist in our galaxy or in neighboring galaxies. Youngsters fantasize about sex to prepare for upcoming experiences which inevitably fall short of their fantasies. Much speculation about happiness bubbles forth for similar reasons.

When we are unhappy, we contemplate happiness, at once longing for it and fearing it. Although most of us have experienced happiness as a fleeting event (from a two-minute kiss to a two-week vacation), we view with suspicion the prospect of sustained happiness.

"If I were happy all the time, I'd be an idiot." Somehow, in our imagination, prolonged happiness and a dull brain go together. Ironically, unhappiness, not happiness, limits our perception and clouds our vision. For example, when we approach a job interview anxiously, we divert a portion of our attention from the present situation, thereby compromising our responses and, perhaps, appearing incoherent or stupid. When we become depressed, we ignore opportunities to change, thereby limiting our possibilities and appearing idiotic in our choices. I have never met a stupid person—only an unhappy one. Dispensing with unhappiness is the single, most significant activity we can undertake in any effort to sharpen our minds and enhance our ability to think. Although we may seek happiness for itself, we may also note that when we are relaxed and comfortable our clarity increases pro-

foundly and we stand flexible and unafraid.

"If I were happy all the time, I'd be a 'limp rag.'" This constitutes another fallacious myth about happiness. The term "limp rag" describes someone who lacks initiative, energy and conviction and who might be easily pushed around and pressured by others. Such a person might withhold fearfully, dull his sensations and live his life without a clear vision to guide him. These characteristics form the portrait of someone dominated by discomfort. In contrast, happiness bubbles forth from an optimistic, hopeful vision of the universe. Unencumbered by the anchor of misery, happier people move decisively and energetically. Even their gentle embrace, their soft smile or their whispered prayer can have great power. Happiness is power! Happiness is self-empowerment.

"If I were happy all the time, I'd probably never move." Some people worry that happiness and lethargy go hand in hand, as if happy people would be without motivation to initiate or participate in human endeavors. Since the cup of happiness would be filled, they reason, we would have no motivation to do anything further. Not so! Instead of using anger, fear, discomfort or jealousy as fuel for action, we would energize ourselves with peace, ease, comfort and excitement and have more reason than ever before to involve ourselves in the pursuits we choose. The happy skier glides more easily down the slope than her fearful counterpart. The happy musician delights enthusiastically in the music he plays, while the

tense artist short-circuits his efforts by fatigue or distress. The happy teacher enjoys passionately the curiosity, the struggles and the victories of her students while her judgmental colleague burns out on her own impatience and annoyance in the classroom. Happy people do not stop moving or participating. On the contrary, their happiness increases their mobility and effectiveness. Instead of fighting fears and running from pain, they see more clearly their wants and move with ease toward them.

"If I were happy all the time, I'd be insensitive." So often we have learned to associate happiness with superficiality and insensitivity. Unhappiness, we believe, signals caring. If someone we love feels sad, we try often to "take on," share or re-create the feeling in ourselves to demonstrate our camaraderie. What we then have is two sad people. If someone we love verbalizes anger about some injustice, we might similarly express anger to show solidarity. What we then have is two angry people. Perhaps, if we stay happy in ourselves, we might ask questions or try in other ways to help someone move through his or her discomfort. Commiserating just supports and amplifies misery. Happiness might, in fact, be the most sensitive and useful tool with which to assist someone we love through a difficult circumstance.

Once, during a discussion which followed a talk that I gave at a conference on attitudinal healing, a woman from the audience used questions about insensitivity to object to my championing happiness as an approach to every situation discussed. She talked about how she and any other reasonable and caring human being would be unhappy if they watched some of the recent television documentaries on starving children. Her tears, she stated, reminded her vividly of her concern. I asked her what she had done in response to her sensitivity to this issue: Had she fed a starving child lately? She looked perplexed for a few moments, then explained that she had given money to United Way. "Don't they feed starving children?" she inquired. Obviously, she did not know.

Later, when I asked the others in the audience who among them got uncomfortable watching such newsreels, almost everyone raised their hand. When I asked who had fed a starving child either directly or indirectly within the last year or two, only a couple of people lifted their hands amid the vast sea of faces.

I shared with them how I, too, used to feel pained by what I believed was the agony of people facing famine and how, like many of them, I never found ways to harness my concern into helpful action. In fact, my own discomfort caused me to turn away. I used to say I could not bear to watch news programs depicting homeless children withered and disfigured by starvation and disease. However, as I became happier, I feared less what I might see. Ultimately, my happiness (as my former unhappy responses had not done) led me to places and situations I would have once systematically avoided. One time, after teaching nurses and nuns in an orphanage in South America how to stimulate emotionally and nutritionally deprived children, Samahria and I walked through a courtyard filled with about sixty boys and girls, some of whom showed obvious signs of malnourishment and abuse. They pounced on us immediately. Some grabbed our legs and arms; others shimmied up our bodies. One little boy climbed up my back and sat squarely on my shoulders. All asked variations of the same question: Would we take them home and be their mother and father? Many people in the audience sighed with sincere and heartfelt pain as they heard of the plight of these children. They judged the situation as terrible. Several indicated how they would never want to be put in a position as untenable as they considered ours.

We had a different reaction to the courtyard scene. We delighted in the energy and daring of these children in their pursuit of a family. How wonderful that they had not lost their spirit and will to survive (and thrive)! We spent hours playing with them and loving them. Because the happiness and gratitude we had chosen to feel opened our eyes to what we could do to help, my wife and I eventually adopted children just like them.

Judging the situation as terrible and responding with un-happiness can short-circuit the efforts and impact of many people who, indeed, care. In contrast, responding from happiness (feeling comfortable and being free of judgments) might prove to be a most empowering, useful and compassionate tool.

All we really want is to be happy. In my work with people over these years, whether they come from the United States, Canada, the Philippines, the Soviet Union, Malaysia, Japan, Sri Lanka, South Africa, France, Belgium, Germany, Nigeria, Mexico, Chile, Israel, Australia, Greece or any other country, I hear beneath the pain, disappointment and discomforts, a powerful wanting to be happy, to be loving and to be loved. This human longing knows no racial or national boundaries. The politics, the relationships, the careers, the finances, the children and the accomplishments become vehicles we use to bring us fulfillment . . . or happiness. Although the individual pursuits are very, very personal and distinctive, the underlying intention draws us all together.

Dialogues to Happiness: One Alternative.

We might call dialogues the second best way to happiness; the first best way, which is the essential focus of this book, would be to decide right now to be happy. However, the second best way has given us invaluable revelations, allowed us to help ourselves and others and, most significantly, helped crystallize our current insights.

In sharing what Samahria and I had learned about the pursuit of happiness, we relied initially and still do rely, in part, on the use of what we call the dialogue process. Simple, gentle, nondirective questions, offered with love and acceptance serve as the fundamental tool. "Why are you angry?" "What's frustrating about her lack of cooperation?" "How does he 'make' you unhappy?" "Why do you believe you're unlovable?" Each question brings a response which stimulates yet another question in an exploration guided by the explorer. The answers and solutions are the explorers', never ours.

In these dialogue sessions, individuals can explore their issues freely and begin to experience themselves as their own best experts. The mentors, those individuals who ask these questions and who have been trained at our teaching center, have spent years with us unearthing and discarding their own judgments. This training enables them to be fully present with a loving, accepting and nonjudgmental attitude during the sessions. This attitude forms the basis of all our work. Without it, questions can often become disguised judgments or accusations. With the attitude, questions can be gentle, useful gifts.

Facilitating others in these inward bound self-exploration sessions has allowed us to see the miracle each person represents. By giving people the opportunity to find their own answers, free of external judgment and pressure, we provide an environment that helps them not only discover resolutions to their concerns, but also to begin nurturing self-acceptance and trusting the wisdom of their own inclinations. As I talked more with people, my reverence for their explorations grew.

I have engaged in dialogues with well-meaning parents, estranged spouses, confused homemakers, delinquent teenagers, burned-out physicians and therapists, stressed executives, discontent senior citizens and people in search of their own spirituality. I have had sessions with child molesters, embezzlers and pathological liars as well as with people who have robbed others, with people who inflicted violence upon friends and strangers and also with those who tried to end their lives by their own hand. In all these sessions I gained a most inspiring insight about all those who passed my way. Every person, I discovered, no matter how objectionable the world viewed their behavior, had been well-intentioned, although a superficial grasp of their situation might lead us to conclude otherwise. *Each person does the best they can in accordance with their beliefs.* Change the beliefs and the resulting feelings and behaviors change. The following story serves to illustrate this point.

Although he had not yet reached his thirtieth birthday, John had been charged three times and convicted once of child-abuse. Following his conviction, he had been separated from his family and incarcerated by court order, but after psychiatric rehabilitation, he had been permitted to return home upon his release from prison. Unfortunately, once again, he attacked his daughter. He described himself as out of control. A trivial incident had led to yet another violent confrontation.

His seven-year-old daughter, Janie, whom he described as

tiny and fragile, had not cleaned the kitchen table after eating. He demanded an explanation. When she started to tremble, obviously frightened, he grabbed her arm with the intent of calming her. Janie pulled away and backed slowly toward the door. She pleaded with him, "Daddy, please don't hurt me." John became furious and commanded her to stop talking and to stop moving away. Janie held her hands up to her quivering lips. "Please, someone help me!" she cried to the empty house as she turned, broke into a full stride and ran down the hallway. He chased her, caught her by the staircase, picked her up off the floor by her head and slammed her brutally against the wall. When she fell, her collarbone snapped in two places and the banister lacerated her face. The impact left her unconscious.

Once he finished his story, which he told in unforgiving detail, John glared at me defensively. He had condemned himself already and just waited for me to concur. If I could have rewritten the past, I would have tried in every way possible to have removed this little girl from harm's way. But the event described to me had occurred. Neither of us could rewrite history, but we could find a useful way to deal with it.

Instead of castigating him as family members, counselors and judges had done, I wanted to love him (be happy with him) in the best way I could. I didn't grimace or form any internal judgments about what he had shared. Since he had concluded his commentary by labeling himself a terrible person, I asked him a simple, nonjudgmental question based on that statement.

"Why do you call yourself a 'terrible' person?" I asked in a soft and easy voice so that he could begin his own gentle inquiry into the nature of his violent actions and the beliefs that fueled them.

He looked at me surprised. "Everyone in the world would call me terrible for what I did."

"Even if that were so," I responded, "we could still ask the question why are *you* calling yourself terrible?"

John peered deeply into my eyes, then sighed. His expression changed; he relaxed his hands, which had been clenched into tight fists on his lap. Perhaps, in that instant, he knew that at least one person on the planet, here and now, could listen to him without responding with anger or disgust.

In an environment of acceptance, John dared to share fears and secrets he had never before been willing to voice to anyone. He itemized the repeated physical assaults of his alcoholic father and the flaunted promiscuity of his mother that persisted throughout his childhood. Each time his daughter failed to obey his instructions explicitly, he concluded her lack of discipline meant she would eventually fill the family mold and, one day, be out of control as he and his parents had so often been. As the dialogue progressed, John began to see that his attacks against his child represented his frightened efforts to save her from his own disturbed vision of a terrifying future based on his past. In unraveling his thought process and belief system, he discovered a motive not unearthed previously. His underlying desire, he saw now, had been to protect his daughter, although his action had been muddled and so very destructive.

He stopped speaking for a long time. His eyes filled with tears. When I asked him what he had been thinking, he said strongly, "I love her. I have always loved her." Those words seemed targeted more for his own ears than mine. He understood in that moment that he had wanted the best for her even as he struggled with his fears. The tight muscles in his jaw flexed as he allowed himself to cry for the first time in ten years.

The single insight that he had been well-intentioned allowed John to let go of so much self-hate and build a new vision of himself based on his acknowledged love for a child he had so blindly trampled. Amid the horror and all that he and others condemned as bad, he had found the seed of something he could identify not only as real, but good. He could now try to reach out to his daughter from a very different place inside.

We spent a total of four afternoons together during which John experienced another person accepting him, loving him and trusting *him* to find his own best answers. No clinical interpretations! No judgments! No advice! John found the insights himself and used those precious four afternoons to change his beliefs, his vision and his life. In the years that followed he never again hit or hurt his little girl, whom he had once loved so fearfully and ineptly. In becoming more self-accepting as well as happier in his actions, he became more capable of nurturing and loving his daughter, giving her an opportunity to heal the wounds he had inflicted.

To really know and understand, firsthand, that people are well intentioned beneath their misery and fear teaches me about the magnificence of human dynamics and enables me to be hopeful. Yes, we could stare with horror at all the "well-intended" souls who use terrorism, drugs, murder and war to fulfill their desires. But we could also know that we are staring into the muddled and explosive face of unhappiness. We can do our very best to prevent such activities, but we can also look upon those around us, no matter how problematic and different they are from us, and acknowledge our common unity obscured by the walls of our own prejudices and judgments. At the core, we all want happiness for ourselves, our children and others we love. We may continue to use different words (peace, contentment, fulfillment, satisfaction, clarity), but the meanings remain the same.

As I have grown to love people, I have developed an awesome respect for their intentions while still questioning freely and without judgments, as best I can, the methods used to fulfill them. The dialogues have become the backbone of a sweet and easy method to help people help themselves to be happier. Each exploration gives people an opportunity to uncover and discard, if they choose, the beliefs fueling their unhappiness and discomfort. But the point of change always occurs in an instant, as it did for John when he discovered (or decided) that his intention toward his daughter had always been sincere and well-meaning.

We can change an idea or thought in a moment of time which can create significant, even irrevocable, shifts in our lives.

Dialogues to happiness worked for Dennis, too, although he extended his journey over a period of weeks. Since his adolescence, he had been very sensitive about his appearance. Although he had married, he could still vividly recall all the girls and women who had declined his invitations for a date. He judged his head to be slightly oversized, his face a bit too long and narrow, his nose too angular and his lips too thin. His receding hairline further damaged his view of himself. He believed others saw him as unappealing and he wrestled with the discomfort and pain such beliefs caused him. In his dialogues Dennis plowed through mountains of self-incriminations. Wherever he turned, he found yet another belief confirming his imperfections. Finally, he realized that any judgments others might have made of him probably reflected in large part his own judgments about himself.

As an experiment, we did a two-hour session in front of mirrors with Dennis exploring and questioning his aesthetics about each and every feature on his face, including the quality of his skin, the wiry hairs of his mustache and the spaces between some of his teeth. He faced himself head-on, then used other mirrors to the side of his head which allowed him to view his left and right profiles. In the end, he laughed, deciding that the most dominant attribute he noticed about his face was his expression. His eyes, nose, cheeks, lips and jaw formed a hundred different faces depending on his attitude and feelings. His smiling face differed profoundly from his frowning face. He expressed excitement about his discovery and decided to be happy with his face and its flexibility. He acknowledged feeling generally more comfortable about himself, while noting that his newfound happiness had not yet been put to the test.

The following Saturday morning after this session, Dennis awakened his eight-year-old daughter gently to prepare for a family outing. Initially, she resisted his prodding, but then bolted upright in bed, full of energy. She grabbed her father, kissed him playfully, then placed her face against his and said, "This would make a great picture!"

Dennis was thrilled. Then, quite innocently, the little girl added, "But it would be a much better picture if it was Mommy's face and mine."

He stroked his daughter's hair, acutely aware of his decision to remain happy despite her comment. He realized that previously he would have been emotionally crushed by it. Now, free of any self-condemnation about his appearance, he could be at peace and open to his child's perspective. So, without hesitation, he asked her a direct question which he would never, ever, have been willing to pose in the past.

"Why would it be better with Mommy's face?"

"Because then," she replied, "you would be taking the picture, and you take better pictures than Mommy."

Opportunities! Opportunities! Questions, more questions and more opportunities! Ultimately, we come to experience questions, when lovingly and nonjudgmentally presented, as magnificent gifts that facilitate our own transformation and help us better understand others.

This might not be the case with questions used to disguise statements and accusations, which many of us have often been bombarded with all our lives. "Why are you always so difficult?" "When will you start behaving properly?" "Can't you ever pick nice friends?" "How could you call what you do a success?" The judgments underlying those words make a commentary most people would easily detect. No wonder we tend to run from questions. Rarely have they been presented to us as a loving gift to help us explore our beliefs and find our own best answers.

———

For one woman, coming for dialogue sessions represented a break with all family traditions. When she was a child, superficial questions had been used like daggers and sincere, personal inquiries had been banned as indecent invasions of privacy. Suzanne had locked herself away behind a barrier of silence. Even so, she admitted loving the attitude of acceptance from the first moment she arrived at our teaching center. Nevertheless, she resisted the questions even while recognizing them as nondirective and nonjudgmental.

Our first sessions together had a unique and delightful stop/start quality. Sometimes, she would remain silent for extended periods. At other times, she would answer questions with an avalanche of words and thoughts, her voice choked with emotions. Much of her discomfort centered around her relationship with her husband and young son. She wanted to control their choices and their actions but had never explored her motives or the impact her overbearing manner had on them. She greeted all disputes with immediate discomfort. Her unwillingness to be open to their protests or requests for discussions had been alienating for everyone in the family. To be here now in this dialogue with me, she insisted, represented a giant step in her life.

As she investigated her need to control what her son wore, I asked her to clarify her reason for wanting that control. She declared that she had no reasons; she just wanted what she wanted. I asked her why she believed that she had no reasons for her actions and her wants.

She looked at me and sighed noisily as we walked along a country road near our Institute. "I don't want you to ask me any more questions."

"Why not?" I inquired, continuing to play my part in our unfolding dialogue.

"There you go! You did it! Listen, if you ask me another question, I'm going to push you into the ditch."

I assessed the depth of the gully beside the road for a moment or two, then asked, "Why, if I ask you another question, would you push me into the ditch?"

Without a moment's hesitation, she shoved me off the side of the road. From my landing place in the shallow ditch, I looked up and asked, "Why do you think you pushed me into this ditch?"

Suzanne started to laugh. "Okay, I'm game. If you can keep asking all those questions, I guess I can answer them . . . all of them." We proceeded with the rest of the session in a much more lively and fluid manner. She had broken through the barrier of her own resistance and now welcomed her exploration. Before we finished, she decided that, rather than get uncomfortable with her husband and son in situations of potential conflict, she would ask questions, trying to make them as neutral as the ones she had heard me ask her. In addition, she would express more by sharing the rationale behind her wants.

The very next day, her son bypassed the overalls she had

put out on his bed, choosing instead to wear dirty jeans. Usually such behavior would have initiated a giant confrontation. However, Suzanne reaffirmed her decision to ask questions, to be open and to be happy. Rather than be combative, she asked her child calmly why he did not wear those "wonderful" overalls. He explained that he could not unbutton the straps of the overalls when he had to go to the bathroom in school. Suzanne stood there amazed, wondering how many other times he had had such sensible and reasonable motives for his actions.

As Edward advanced toward his late fifties, he slid deeper and deeper into a depression that sucked the enthusiasm out of all his life endeavors. Psychotherapy and medication had had no visible effects. As we explored his concerns in an extended dialogue, he raised three major issues that disturbed him profoundly and continuously, all of which he insisted he must resolve in order to improve his outlook and general state of health. First, he felt stalled in his career with few options for advancement left. Second, his marriage had become strained as a result of growing friction between him and his wife. And finally, he noted, with great concern, his sexual potency had diminished dramatically in the last three years.

As he itemized his problems, he decided if he could at least resolve just one of them now, during this dialogue, he could consider his time well spent. When he explored his relationship with his wife, he protested her lack of emotional availability and her lack of sexuality. Initially, he blamed her for his current difficulties, but, in the end, he let go of judging her. In fact, he spent a few moments reaffirming his love for her in spite of the present difficulties. Accessing those feelings surprised him since he had long ago dismissed the idea he would ever talk about love with any degree of enthusiasm. Before he moved to another subject, he noted that any change of attitude on his part regarding this issue still did not resolve the problems in his marriage. However, he admitted, he felt a touch more comfortable.

After sifting through practical options available to him in business, he groaned about all the obvious inequities. "Life is unfair!" he barked. Then he smiled shyly, reflecting on his comment. "So, do I fight the universe or take it as it comes?"

"What do you want to do?" I asked.

"Stop fighting," he declared, sighing noisily before continuing. "But, Bears, because I decided to give up doing battle doesn't mean my business issues are resolved . . . far from it! I've just shifted my position a bit . . . that's all." Although Edward's depression seemed to be lifting right before my eyes, he undercut the value of every attitudinal shift by prioritizing problem solving.

When we discussed sexual potency, he focused on his beliefs and judgments about aging. Had he become old before his time? When he reviewed all his limitations and capabilities, he could see some advantages to growing older. He surprised himself by cataloging all the new activities he had come to enjoy. He smiled fleetingly, then reassured me that we still had not uprooted his underlying sexual problem. Nevertheless, his expression had dramatically softened.

Edward asked if we could sit quietly for a few minutes in the gazebo near the pond on the Institute property. As we sat facing each other, he gazed at the rolling lawns around us, the majestic oak trees in rows along the road and the stately mountain looming nearby. Although we had walked the area for hours, he hadn't noticed the lovely landscape. "It's beautiful," he whispered, then he turned his gaze toward me now and smiled again. "I feel real good." He paused as if reviewing his own words. "I do. But this doesn't make any sense; I haven't resolved any of my problems."

"Do you have to resolve your problems or issues in order to feel good?" I asked him.

"I always thought so," he said softly. "So if I could feel better when nothing in the world has changed, what happened?"

"What do you think?"

"This is going to sound funny. The issues are the same, but I've changed my attitude. Somehow I'm not allowing those problems to be as important as before. I guess I don't have to resolve them to feel better. What a relief!" He nodded his head. "I feel relaxed. I feel I can even enjoy the beautiful views all around us. I feel I can enjoy you, too, and your questions." Tears filled his eyes. "It's like a miracle."

Edward's life did change as a result of his many small attitudinal shifts during the session. What he called a miracle, he, himself, had created. He had changed some beliefs, dropped some judgments and altered his vision. He had empowered change by *choosing* to see the same old problems differently.

Nothing had changed, yet everything had changed!

One afternoon, several years ago, I did a three-hour dialogue session with a thirty-seven-year-old woman who had been intensely unhappy for most of her adult life. Although she arrived visibly distressed, she jumped into the exploration process with great enthusiasm, answered every question I posed, and unraveled with amazing skill the entire interlocking network of beliefs that fueled her anger and fears. She dissected them carefully, one by one, then proceeded to dump them like old clothing.

When our time drew to a close, Cindy smiled brightly and said confidently, "I did it all. I'm finished. I really am! I'm free to be happy now!"

Wanting to give her the space to arrive at her own conclusions, I did not offer any comment, though inside I found myself concurring. I had never seen anyone explore with such clarity. Yes, indeed, it appeared to me, too, that she had uncovered and settled all the issues which supported her unhappiness. Awesome. Finished in three hours and, as she herself claimed, "free to be happy now!"

Cindy sprang to her feet and walked energetically to the door. Suddenly, she stopped and stood motionless for a few moments, her hand clasping the door knob. Then, she turned slowly and said self-consciously, "What time next week?"

Although the sessions continued for almost four months, Cindy never did anything more than rehash and juggle the contents of her first session. At the conclusion of the entire process, she shared with me the belief that had stopped her from putting into practice all that she had learned during our very first encounter.

"If I could work out thirty-seven years of misery in a short three hours, then I would have had to be a greater fool all my life than I could ever have imagined. If the answers had been so accessible, why hadn't I found them sooner?" Her underlying belief: big problems require big solutions, all of which take time to formulate and enact. Four months to be exact! After she had spent what she considered enough time rechecking and rearranging beliefs to warrant changing patterns perfected over thirty-seven years, she gave herself permission to change, knowing full well that she had had all the data in the first session and could have acted upon it. Next time, she

promised herself, change would not take so long. She even
entertained the possibility of changing in an instant.

Questions presented sincerely and without a hidden agenda
can facilitate the most provocative changes in ourselves and
build bridges of clarity and love to others. We can do dialogues, acknowledging them as magnificent tools, and be
grateful to have the time and opportunity to explore and
change beliefs (one belief at a time if necessary) which fuel
unhappiness, and to move ultimately toward being happier.
But we can also cut to the heart of the matter and recognize
the power and immediacy of our decisions and choices (to be
happy, to stay happy, to be open, to ask questions, to answer
questions, to change behavior), whether those decisions and
choices occur within or outside of a dialogue. We can leap
over the "working" portion of the process and adopt a vision
that helps us implement our happiness option now.

Happiness In an Instant: Another Alternative.

Beetle fossils from two million years ago indicate ancient
beetles were not significantly different from those of today.
Bowfin fish have remained almost the same for over one
hundred million years. Sturgeons, turtles, ants and alligators
also demonstrate long-term stability. Evolution at best, Dar-

winian paleontologists used to argue, occurs gradually, little by little. However, although they had vast collections of fossils with which to document the many small changes, they had some huge gaps in their findings. Apparently, some creatures disappear abruptly and unexpectedly off the face of the earth while others pop into existence just as unexpectedly. In addition, within a given species, scientists noted primitive life forms suddenly coexisting with more developed versions of the same life form. Researchers used to believe the lack of transition from one version of a life form to another could be explained by lack of definitive research data. But, recently, as a result of having more detailed and complete information, they have formed dramatically different conclusions. In spite of some evolving changes within species, nature does continually bring into existence new and different creatures with no forebears. These new designs and advances in organisms occur suddenly.

Rebirthing ourselves into happy and loving people who do not use pain and suffering to grow would be analogous to popping new creatures into existence. We can demonstrate this different design and coexist with the earlier version of the human form as a celebration and a teaching of what's possible. The precedence of instant change has been set by nature and we are nature's children.

Our happiness, as well as the beliefs and visions that support it, has as much substance as any physical reality currently in the universe. The human organism is not simply a lifeless heap into which the soul breathes life. We can put aside the antiquated view of body separate from mind and replace it with a more valid perception—bodymind! Although it has become more fashionable to view the human organism as a series of interrelated systems (cardiovascular system, lymph system, central nervous system, autonomic nervous system, the endocrine system, the immune system) more recent scientific revelations suggest a bodymind connection more comprehensive and powerful than any previously conceived. Thoughts, and indeed their associated feelings, have an immediate material component that comes alive throughout the body and creates an instantaneous cellular network far more intricate and whole than the "hard" wiring of the neurological system. Thinking has physical substance in the form of neurotransmitters and neuropeptides, visible chemical substances which are not confined to the brain but operate bodywide. The brain no longer is the single seat of thinking. The body dynamic suggests that the immune system, the intestines, the liver, the kidneys and endless other sites produce the chemistry of thoughts continuously and simultaneously (as we think).

In creating new thoughts or revising old ones, we change the actual physiology of the entire body system in an instant.

Atoms and molecules realign and readjust immediately. New biochemical and cellular configurations pop into existence.

The mind is everywhere, and we can change ourselves dramatically and profoundly by simply changing our minds.

Happiness Versus Truth

A couple in search of a more effective method to help their special child came with him to The Option Institute to participate in an individualized program. Mom was a psychoanalyst. Dad was a philosophy professor at a major university. They had had difficulty accepting their situation and finding help for their stricken son. Their pilgrimage from hospital to hospital left them confused and depressed. Would their child be damned by his handicap and dysfunction forever? They loved their son but felt blinded by their own unhappy response to his condition. Their educational prowess, their razor-sharp intellects and pungent wits had not unlocked the door to this problem.

I shared some experiences we had had working with families and the discovery that even after doing many explorations and dialogues intended to help make issues clear, I had come to realize that all change came from a decision to change—a decision made in an instant. Before I taught this process, I had believed that changing myself was painful and a rather lengthy procedure. In my own studies and independent pursuits, the idea of "no pain, no gain" had once guided all my endeavors. I did not realize at the time that those beliefs had become self-fulfilling prophecies: I had made my own changes slow and painful. However, that mode of thinking gave way finally to a very different awareness. I noticed whenever I did actually make a change (stopped smoking, began to diet, let go of anger), I had, just moments before, made a decision to alter my behavior. In effect, I decided to choose differently. Thus, I could either spend my life "processing" (which certainly could be helpful and enlightening) or maximize my power of choice and make change an instantaneous experience. I eventually chose the latter and, whether through dialogues or active decision making, began to watch others do the same.

Soon our discussion focused on the impact that beliefs and attitude had had on our life experiences and life embrace. Both parents wanted to hear more about the idea of beliefs as self-fulfilling prophecies.

"If we view a condition as hopeless and incurable," I suggested, "we deal with it accordingly. We don't try to educate someone we believe to be uneducable."

They had no dispute with that perspective, but wondered whether they had failed as parents by believing and acting as if their child's condition was hopeless for all these years. When I questioned what they meant by "failed as parents," the mother smiled and said, "I know I don't have to accuse myself of being a failure. I've worked on changing that since I have been here. But, Bears, am I supposed to be comfortable and happy with the situation with my son? I'm not sure I want to be. And even if I did, I don't think I could quite manage any immediate change in my perspective and responses; my husband and I would probably need two lifetimes to work on it."

"Hummm . . . Two lifetimes?" I murmured respectfully, "That's a long time." I leaned forward, touched their hands lightly, smiled and said I wanted to tell them a story about a recent occurrence in my life in which I decided to create my perspective and design my responses, as well as change them, on a moment-to-moment basis.

While I had been engaged in a dialogue session with a married couple, a staff member summoned me, a rare and singular event. We never interrupt our work with people except in the case of absolute emergency. Nancy led me down the hall and informed me that the police had just called, asking that I come immediately. My son, Raun, had been in an automobile accident just up the road, and, although they didn't think he had been injured seriously, they nevertheless wanted me to come to him now.

After excusing myself, I jumped into my car, drove north as instructed and remembered another phone call I had received of a similar nature over twenty years before. A nurse who had stayed with my mother during her final, painful bout with cancer telephoned to tell both my father and me that my mother had had a seizure and although she seemed stable, the woman suggested we come home immediately. What the nurse did not tell us was that my mother had, in fact, already died. I could anticipate the same scenario now with my son, but I realized I could also choose not to paint pictures in my mind of landscapes I could not see. I jettisoned the memory and decided to focus all my energy on staying absolutely present with driving my vehicle safely. No past. No future. Only this moment with my hands guiding the steering wheel and my eyes locked on the unfolding road. Time became a physical sensation as if it had been stretched. Although I was driving fast, I could detect minute details of the surrounding fields and meadows as if they rolled before me in slow motion. The trees and wild flowers abutting the road appeared painted from an intensely vivid palette. Through the open car window the wind hummed in my ears like a whispering chorus.

As my vehicle reached the crest of a hill, I could see the flashing turrets of police cars and an ambulance that blocked the road. My eyes scanned the scene of the accident, searching without success for my son's car. After I stopped by the roadside, I catapulted myself into the street and began to sprint toward a crowd of people. In that moment, I noticed a crushed vehicle overturned in a ditch beside the road. Its wheels faced the sky. The battered brown paint of the driver's door identified the car as my son's. As I pushed through the crowd of people, a man grabbed my arm, walking with me as if he knew me, and said in a very studied voice, "We don't think it's as bad as it looks. We're just taking precautions."

No matter what I was about to see, I wanted only to be helpful to my son and I knew that I had to remain clear and present in order to be helpful and useful. I could feel myself deciding in each moment to affirm and reaffirm that intention.

Several people moved aside as I approached an opening in the crowd. In the middle of this group of people, three medics worked steadily on a person who sat braced in a metal chair. His bandaged head and eyes were encased in a steel cage, his neck and torso enclosed in a full body brace. His arms were strapped to the menacing armor and his legs tied together. Through the metal apparatus and surgical gauze, I recognized my son. I could feel my love for him oozing out my fingertips as I tried to ingest the implications of what I saw. Had he sustained some massive spinal injury? I felt neither panicked nor elated. I stood at a crossroad inside. I could quite easily see the worst and scream or I could be hopeful, present and useful.

Once I reached Raun, I knelt down by his side, touched his hands gently and told him that I was now with him. He whispered a shaky "Okay." When I asked him how he felt, he mumbled about not feeling much of anything and seemed anxious about not being able to remember what had happened. I asked the medics if his head had been hit. The answer was affirmative. What about his eyes? I asked why his eyes had been bandaged. The paramedics said that in their haste to secure his head in the brace with the gauze, they had inadvertently covered his eyes, which had not been injured. I worked my fingers though the metal rods and rolled the bandage back. Raun looked at me cautiously, his eyes glazed. I stroked his skin with the tips of my fingers and smiled at him. He reported now that both his head and neck hurt and wanted to know if other parts of his body had been injured.

While the attendants monitored his vital signs, I suggested we could experiment, which might give him more information. He said weakly, "Go ahead." I held his fingers in my hands and instructed him to move them. Though he seemed to be in shock, he understood me. And yet, his hands did not move. I made the request a second time while staring intently at his limbs. Finally, very slowly, he began to move the thumb and index finger of his left hand. Could he move the fingers of his other hand? He did. Then I asked him to move his toes. I grabbed his sneakers to see if I could feel the movement. Again, nothing happened. When I looked up, he peered at me wide-eyed. He couldn't move his feet. I told him not to be concerned; we would play this game again later. His eyes filled with tears. Then, quite suddenly, as I began removing my hands from his shoes, his toes pushed up hard against the nylon material.

Once they had loaded him into the ambulance, they began communicating his vital signs to the hospital. I sat beside him, held on to his hands so he could feel me with him and bent over so I could look directly into his eyes. I could see his panic. More than anything in that moment, I wanted to help him with his fear. I did not know whether these would be my last moments with my son, but, whatever happened, I wanted them to be the best. Somewhere deep inside I could observe myself making one decision after another.

"Raun," I said from a profoundly quiet place inside, "while we're taking this ride to the hospital, there is something we can do, you and I, together. Although we don't know what's happening inside your body right now, we can fill ourselves and this ambulance with our gratitude. You're alive! And Raun, we have this time together. We can be grateful for that." I could feel a river of ease and wonder wash through my body like a warm summer rain. Each moment became fixed in my mind as a precious gift. "Raun, we can also try to help your body do the best it can for itself. If you put yourself in a relaxed, peaceful place, you'll free all the energy inside for healing that might have been used up by being scared or tight. Okay?"

"Okay," Raun said softly, obviously still panicked.

"Great," I responded. "Firstly, you and I know something about being relaxed. It's not magical. We can do it anytime. We just have to decide to make it our major priority and do it. So why don't we start there—with you deciding to relax."

Raun squeezed my hands, inhaled a deep breath, then sighed noisily. The tension in his face dissipated completely as tears filled his eyes once again and a smile softened his lips.

For the next twenty minutes I led him, and myself too, in a relaxing meditation. Although I had guided others in visualizations and meditations in my work over the years, I do not recall ever before coming from such a deep, happy and peaceful place inside. Neither of us knew how serious or life-threatening his internal injuries might be. Yet, during the entire ambulance ride, we experienced only serenity and the most supportive bond between us. Once again, the lesson was clear. I could choose my vision and my attitude. The gift of that awareness allowed me to be helpful and useful to my son. I could think of no greater blessing. Raun, too, had the same experience of "deciding." One evening after dinner, some-time following his release from the hospital with no serious injury, he walked up to me, threw his arms around me (not the traditional move of a teen-age boy) and said: "I love you, Dad."

Squeezing him close, I asked, "How come you said that?"

"When they put me into the ambulance," he said, "I felt so scared. When you leaned over and said we could be grate-ful and relaxed, everything changed. I realized that, yeah, I could feel that way even then if I wanted to—and I did. I am really learning a lot." He smiled and hugged me a second time.

When I concluded my story, the psychoanalyst and her philosopher husband nodded for a few seconds. Then the wife continued her protest.

"Actually, I loved your story, Bears, but it's anecdotal, not a scientific study. You, your wife and the others on your staff keep talking about feelings, attitudes and happiness as decisions. You just decide! I guess your story could be a powerful example of deciding or choosing to feel a certain way. But you talk as if we have complete control, as if any of us could decide to change anything we think or feel . . . just like that," she said as she snapped her fingers. "If you study the great psychological thinkers, their findings are quite the opposite. In analysis, I work with people for four years, five years, sometimes more. The work is often difficult and painful. Some patients change some thoughts and behaviors, but not all. And even when they change, they do so in small reasonable steps and not necessarily completely. Not quite the total re-creation you talk about. People have their pasts; they have to contend with their childhood histories. You just don't wipe that away. You learn to cope with it better . . . and that's the success." She paused for a moment, looked at her husband for a fleeting moment, then turned back to me. "This whole idea that you could change yourself on the basis of a decision or a series of decisions, that you could re-create yourself simply by choosing new beliefs and a new attitude—did you ever consider that you might be wrong?"

I leaned back, startled by the simplicity and directness of her question. "I don't mean to sound arrogant," I answered, "but no . . . I never really thought about what we were teaching as being 'wrong.' But give me a minute. I would like to consider it now."

The philosopher crossed his arms in front of his chest and regarded me rather sweetly. His wife smiled, resting her case. They gave me time, never pressing for an answer as I mulled over this possibility. Finally, I responded.

"Okay," I suggested cautiously. "Suppose I am wrong. You and the philosophers and psychoanalysts are right. Suppose it takes a long time to change and you can only change small parts of yourself, and the whole process is very difficult. However, I don't know that truth. I have been thinking and acting as if change can occur in an instant, as a choice, and the process doesn't even have to be painful. In addition, I have this silly idea that we can change everything, absolutely everything, about ourselves. Now, holding these untruths, I act on them and choose differently for myself and then give myself the experience of changing dramatically. Nothing about who I am today seems logically connected to the unhappiness, anxiety and confusion that once permeated most of my every waking hour. Now, observing these changes in me and entertaining these new ideas, my wife adopts this same unrealistic perspective that she, too, can choose different beliefs and change her life as well. She then has the same experience of quick and binding transformation. Several years later, we apply this same erroneous notion to helping our son reverse a supposedly incurable illness. Then we start teaching this incorrect belief about the power each of us has to change quickly and be happier to other people and they, too, alter lifelong attitudes and behavior patterns in profound and immediate ways. Wow! So what we might have here is you holding the truth and being 'right' and us teaching something that's possibly false, no matter how helpful and healing. And yet it's definitely changed my life and the lives of many others in rather marvelous and wondrous ways. We feel truly blessed to be happier, more loving, more at peace and more powerful in our everyday interactions.

"As you've indicated," I continued, "you've experienced and continue to experience a lot of misery in your life and yet, you have what you call the 'truth.' Well then, so much for the 'truth,' I'd rather be happy!"

Happiness and the belief that we can experience our own happiness, anytime and anyplace, is the ultimate attitudinal advantage!

IV · Thriving in a "User-Friendly" Universe

As we gaze into the universe deep inside of us, and into the universe which surrounds us, we search for an answer to the question—is it friendly?

BNK

Teaching everything in terms of circles or wheels is a Native American spiritual tradition. The "mistakes wheel" is a new perspective on the medicine wheel, which is part of the Sweet Medicine Path, and shares the keys to self-acceptance and acceptance of the universe. The five sections of the disk hold five messages about mistakes.

In the north part of the wheel, the message reads: "Learning from our own mistakes." In the west part, it's: "Learning from the mistakes of others." In the east portion, it says: "Learning from the mistakes of our teachers," and, in the south segment, it's: "Being willing to make as many mistakes as it takes."

Finally in the center of this medicine wheel, a position which represents the essence of the learning, the following is written: "Learning that there is no such thing as a mistake."

If we open ourselves to the possibilities that all we encounter and do offers us opportunities for joy and learning, then we can make all circumstances useful and fruitful. Certainly, a universe in which such a possibility exists would be "user-friendly." It might, in fact, be even more friendly than we could have ever imagined.

As belief-makers, we can create any vision of the universe we want and then accumulate evidence to support it. In choosing the happiness option, and the attitudinal advantage which flows from it, we open a window to the world that reveals a wonderful and supportive environment. However, while we marvel at what we see, our more pessimistic and skeptical voice might jeer at us from the sidelines. So rather than indulge immediately in fascinating perusals of evidence suggesting a "user-friendly" universe, we might begin by confronting and dispensing with the alarmist in us, by first acknowledging and even amplifying its voice.

Suppose we begin by painting a bleak picture. We can easily anticipate disaster and support our expectations by citing the scientific theory called the Second Law of Thermodynamics which suggests that the universe, as it cools, becomes more and more disordered. Slowly but surely, we can plot in human terms an inescapable plunge into chaos. The protective ozone shield around the earth will disintegrate; the dangerous warming associated with the "greenhouse" effect will increase; natural resources will be depleted; water and food will be poisoned by human refuse; war and terrorism will flourish; buildings will decay and collapse, and people will grow old, fall prey to disease and die. If, somehow, the human race survives such adversity, someone can always remind us that the sun, whose fuel resources decline each year, will inevitably cool and dim, resulting in the death of all life on this planet. Finally, if we search for the ultimate dismal perspective, we can cite a popular scientific hypothesis of the universe which suggests the "big bang" of creation approximately eighteen billion years ago will end with a collapse into the "big crunch," resulting in total annihilation. Creatures, places, planets, galaxies, even time and space, will disappear!

What can we do in the face of such a "gloom and doom" portrait? We could dismiss this picture as fallacious because it lacks some very crucial ingredients—you, me and happiness. Initially, such a response might sound naive and preposterous. However, we help design the universe with our perceptions and actions. Our consciousness and our wants count! Therefore, we can create a very different portrait and play the game of finding evidence to provide a thoughtful basis for a contrasting optimistic world vision.

Consider the demonstrated and potential power of the

human race. In probing space, our species have expanded our reach, leaving the moon and other nearby planets altered by our visits and our exploratory equipment. At home we have changed the face of the earth by erecting physical structures across almost every landscape. When buildings fall down, we construct new and stronger ones. When an accident severs a hand from an arm, we perform sophisticated microsurgery to reconnect the two. As people die, babies are born. Though we still fight wars in some areas, we have maintained and expanded the peace in others.

Through our easy use of telephones, airplanes and communication satellites, we have united humankind into a global village, allowing people to share scientific and medical technology as well as social, political and spiritual ideas. People in one country sing songs to raise money to feed people in other countries. Conscious concern for human and environmental ecology has become a formidable force in helping all of us to respect and create safeguards for all life.

Even the old vision of a physical universe of extreme violence, characterized by galaxies shooting through space and by impending intergalactic collisions, has been replaced by a profoundly different and more accurate insight. We can now document an observable universe of expanding space. The discovery that galaxies are at rest, each in an ever-expanding and inflating "bubble," suggests an amazingly flexible universe continuously "making room" to accommodate growth and change harmoniously. No danger here of immense astro-catastrophies or haphazard cataclysms. On the contrary, we can discern a brilliantly choreographed dance in space.

Which series of explanations about the universe represent the truth? Neither. Explanations and evidence do not constitute truth; they merely uphold or verify someone's position. In a court of law, truth remains illusive while evidence or proof becomes the deciding factor. The ultimate and accepted truth is simply what the jury decides to believe. For that reason, the innocent can be jailed and the guilty go free. What we can prove or can't prove becomes far more significant than the reality of the event. Our perception of the world, ultimately, defines it—and we feel and act accordingly.

Therefore, choosing our perception or vision has profound practical impact (legal cases, career choices, political posturing, parenting and such) as well as profound spiritual impact. For example, to embrace a "gloom and doom" universe means, by inference, to choose a rather unsupportive creation and creator. However, we can resolve this dilemma without even "disproving" the evidence of pessimists. We can let go of our judgments about depleted ozone layers, pollution and a burnt-out sun and be inclined, even in the face of such possibilities, to view the future as neither good nor bad but just evolving. Some might see such a view as requiring a mighty intellectual stretch; but we can make it.

If we do, in an instant, we dismantle "gloom and doom," replacing it simply with "what is." Taking such a stance, we could call the creator, or God, impartial.

However, we could seek and discover evidence for an even more exciting and hopeful vision—that of a user-friendly universe. To choose such a vision would be to choose a God biased in our favor, one who set the universe in motion to support us and our wants. A universe so conceived would be hospitable to people's striving to be happy (to love and be loved, to be at peace and to be inspired by life's possibilities).

If none of the above views is necessarily more valid than the other, how do we choose our perspective? Easy! First, we take the risk out of our decision-making by remembering the message of the medicine wheel. "There is no such thing as a mistake." Therefore, whatever we decide, we cannot make a "wrong" choice! Second, we ask ourselves which perspective serves us and our happiness or which perspective pleases us.

In my life, I have chosen the user-friendly perspective including a belief in a happy and loving God trying to help me be happy and loving. So much of my early religious training and later studies championed pain and suffering not only as a necessary and inevitable ingredient of life, but also as a genuine curative and enlightening pathway to holding hands with a supreme being. Although I can say I have learned from pain, I have grown so much more from happiness. Although I can point to suffering as an ingredient I mixed into my search for a more spiritual awareness, I recognize that my increased inner ease, self-acceptance and happiness has allowed me a profound spiritual embrace not available in the midst of my desperation and discomfort.

In choosing a user-friendly vision of the universe, I have noticed more supportive action and opportunities around me. In choosing happiness, I have encountered a happy God. In choosing love, I have encountered a loving God.

I have never regretted these choices. In fact, the more I deepen my conviction about a user-friendly universe, the more evidence materializes that leads me to believe such a perspective is valid and true. But then again, I know some funny things about evidence, validity and truth.

Some Playful Concepts, Observations and Data in Support of a User-Friendly Universe.

Over twenty years ago, a British scientist proposed a vision of the planet scoffed at by most of those who heard it. Could it be, he speculated, that the earth is a giant creature, a fantastic organism that lives, adjusts and readjusts itself through all of its offspring? Rather than viewing plants and animals as distinct from rocks and gravel, he proposed a very different vision of the earth as an evolving creature who has spawned a seemingly infinite variety of forms and phenomena (water, soil, insects, plants, fish, invertebrates, mammals, fire, electricity, skyscrapers) which have interacted and matured together as brothers and sisters.

He named his visionary creature "Gaia" and suggested there was much to learn from seeing our home as an organic and self-regulating system with interrelated, mutually supportive parts. When viewed from a telecommunications satellite or the photographic eye of a space probe, the earth appears to be one magnificent swirling mass of changing phenomena. The gigantic oceans, the sculptured land areas, the atmosphere above and the creatures below merge into a single life form, no differently from the way fifty trillion separate cells of the human body merge to create highly individualized internal/external landscapes (hands, feet, stomach, bones, intestine, blood vessels) which, in turn, interconnect and act in unison as a single organism. The concept of Gaia suggests a profound level of communion among all life forms and phenomena on the planet.

Suddenly, in their search for a greater understanding of the ecosystem of the planet and its crust, scientists turn now to this once wild vision of Gaia and grasp for a new, more useful and uplifting perspective of themselves and the environment they inhabit.

In 1665, a Dutch scientist discovered something quite star-tling. If he took two pendulum clocks, each a different size and made of different materials and placed them on a wall in close proximity to each other, they would begin to alter their rhythms subtly until they beat in perfect unison. More re-cently, scientists have found that two heart cells, taken from two different living creatures on the planet, when put near each other under the microscope, will synchronize and start beating together despite the space between the cells.

Similarly, mothers and daughters, female friends and women living together often report noticing that their men-strual cycles begin to occur simultaneously as if their internal body rhythms were synchronized. Novel experiments have illustrated that people near one another, but not in visual contact, will yawn within seconds of each other.

If a diverse group of people, including a newborn infant, occupies a room in which a radio or stereo system plays music with a distinct melody and strong beat, many in the group, including the infant, will move their feet and fingers to the music. Some might rock their torsos or move their heads. It could be said that these people are "entraining" themselves to the rhythms and motions around them.

Recently, I watched a film documentary celebrating the birthday of Dr. Martin Luther King. During each gathering and each march captured on film, someone inevitably began to sing "We Shall Overcome," the anthem of the civil rights movement in the United States. Soon, several others began to sing, then twenty others, finally hundreds participated. People joined arms and rocked back and forth as they sang together. The easy synchronism created its own momentum and energy. Interestingly, in each segment of film, I noted a few people in the group who did not sing. Their nonparticipation for whatever their personal motives, demonstrated that entrainment and synchronization involves choice. We can decide to participate or not participate; however, observation suggests an inclination and willingness to experience the rhythms of those around us.

All life forms pulsate, but why the tendency to do it together? Why do we mimic the tempo of music even at birth? Why do women in close relationships develop similar bodily cycles? Why do separate heart cells or pendulum clocks, in close proximity, synchronize their beat? What force determines such a propensity for harmony? What common energy moves all living creatures so strongly toward synergistic interaction? Some call it intelligence; others recognize it as God. Whatever the speculation, it appears to be friendly.

We can perceive our environment as harsh, challenging or even hostile to life, but we can also perceive the adaptability and perfect suitability of all aspects of nature. As we rush to judge life as a struggle, we miss the obvious wonder of human beings and the other creatures of this planet. All life forms that exist here do so because they not only can survive; they can thrive. The black bears of northern Minnesota, for instance, provide an insightful example not of struggling but of suitability and harmonious adaptation.

The subzero winters of northern Minnesota create a frozen, inhospitable landscape. But the black bears who live there have a simple remedy for their cold climate; they sleep through it. They are the champions of hibernation; they nap for almost seven months a year, depending on the weather.

What they do during their extended slumber is unique and exciting. They lower their body temperature, which slows down their metabolism, so they no longer require any water or food other than what their own stored body fats provide for survival during this extended period. In addition, they do not urinate or defecate. In fact, their body system changes, enabling them to leach the urine from their system internally, convert it while they sleep into protein and transport the new "food" to their own internal organs and muscles to rejuvenate and build new tissues. As a result, when they arise after approximately seven months of slumber, they are toned, agile and immediately capable of caring for themselves. The amazing flexibility of their internal organs as these animals greet changing seasons suggests body mechanics that are quite user-friendly.

———

Most plants and trees grow toward the sun. The mighty oaks and redwoods stand tall and lift their trunks straight toward the sky. Nevertheless, when I have climbed to the tops of mountains and walked along virgin seashores, whether in the United States, Europe or South America, I have always been fascinated by the uniquely twisted and irregular growth of trees in these areas. Many appear gnarled, others stooped and bent. I remember once reading a poem which eulogized these "sad" forms as "beaten" by the wind into shriveled submission. Ah, but are they "beaten into submission" by the wind? A very different understanding emerges from studies of the growth patterns of such trees. If a tree is exposed to a fierce prevailing wind, instead of growing upward in opposition to the force, it adjusts its growth pattern in harmony with the wind. As new cells develop, they build a trunk with a configuration compatible to the wind rather than resistant to it. What some might depict as a struggle is actually the silent inner dance of a tree moving synergistically with the wind in a demonstration of perfect harmony and suitability.

As a young boy, I used to look skyward in amazement as flocks of migratory birds flew north or south depending on the season. Without exception, they gathered in massive "V" formations in the sky. I always wanted to know why they did this. My great curiosity led me to create myths to explain their flights. Sometimes, I would sweep my hands above my head in great arcs to the left or right and think I noticed the birds regrouping. I imagined the invisible hand of God reaching through the clouds and guiding these birds as a salute to the other creatures on the planet.

Only as an adult did I come to learn more about such flights and their meaning. When a bird cuts through the air, she creates in her wake an uplift or updraft. When a second bird locks into position behind the first bird at approximately a forty-five degree angle, he can take advantage of the updraft and glide through the air with less effort. In fact, he will be able to go faster and farther with greater ease. In such formations, birds can actually extend their flights seventy percent farther than if they had been flying alone. By coordinating their movement, they create a synergy, whereby their accumulated efforts produce a total mileage far greater than had they flown separately.

Now you might ask: "What happens to the poor bird in the front of that 'V' formation?" I asked the same question too. The birds keep changing the nose of the "V" so at different times there are different lead birds, enabling previous leaders to take advantage of the other birds' updrafts. Their cooperative efforts are not only mutually supportive, but create a single force greater than the sum of their parts. A hostile environment or a user-friendly one?

Scientific studies of the grazing patterns of animals render obsolete the notion that different species must compete and fight over the same food. On an African savannah, researchers observed that while one species ate the long dry stems of grasses, another herd of different animals grazing on the same plain munched only on the side-shoots of the grasses. Also, to the scientists' surprise, a third species which grazed the same area at a later time ate only ground-hugging plants and other plant parts. All these animals appeared perfectly suited to their niche in the food web and instinctively respectful of the other creatures with whom they shared the habitat.

The human body can certainly be viewed as a user-friendly apparatus. Self-propelled, self-regulating and self-regenerating, the human creature epitomizes one of nature's most complex creations, capable of performing thousands of distinct yet coordinated and mutually supportive functions.

Our heart pumps, our blood circulates, our lungs breathe, our brain fires neurons, our glands secrete hormones, our stomach metabolizes food, our kidneys process urine, our liver filters blood, macrophages consume bacteria, lymphocytes neutralize viruses and endless other operations occur simultaneously without our conscious effort or awareness. Oftentimes, physicians and other concerned individuals, in their vigilance for what can go wrong in the human system, neglect to acknowledge and celebrate all that goes "right." Even in the face of disease, the body can rally its multiple support systems and persevere.

Pursuing any aspect of our bodymind can dazzle us with the nature of creation that weaves through the very fabric of who we are. The ability to hear might be one example among many. A faint sound will move the eardrum back and forth only 40 billionths of an inch (only ten times the diameter of the smallest atom). This minute movement activates the lever action of three tiny bones, whose action magnifies the pressure on the fluid of the inner ear twenty-two times. This force, in turn, vibrates 24,000 tiny hairlike structures of varying length. Only those hairs resonant to a given pitch move. The vibration of these structures triggers responses in attached nerve cells which send messages to the brain. Our brain then deciphers the signals, distinguishing subtle variations of tone, pitch and texture so exquisitely that we can identify a vast multitude of sounds: voices, vehicles, machines, music and so forth. The process occurs as an easy continuum. What universe or God could have created such sensitive, sophisticated and useful equipment? The answer: a friendly one!

Our creation of a new world picture, which would be supportive of us and therefore our pursuit of happiness, begins with attentiveness to our own human magnificence and to the innate tendency we and other creatures have to move together in like or compatible rhythms. At the same time, we can also acknowledge and applaud our power to choose either to move with surrounding rhythms or to be independent of them. We can notice the miracle of suitability and adaptability of creatures to their environment as well as the demonstrated communion among living species, plants, even the wind, as they create a habitat of mutual support.

We plant the seeds of a user-friendly universe with our perception: "The eye sees what it brings to seeing."

V · Nothing Is Impossible

These are the days of miracles and wonder.

PAUL SIMON

When we share our work with people, they typically ask for the "miracle" stories: the cerebral palsied child who gained dramatic control over her limbs; the suicidal young woman who uncovered her passion for living; the stroke victim who defied his doctor's prognosis and learned to walk; the father who found the courage to return home after abandoning his family years earlier; the cancer patient who embraced a new attitude and whose cancer went into remission. We can celebrate, as we do, and be inspired by the power in each person to make such changes. However, our awareness suggests that the real miracles lie elsewhere and are perhaps less apparent, though equally powerful. What amazes us most is that these people have chosen to make happiness and love tangible in their lives.

Then why, I asked myself, did audiences at lectures, television interviewers and reporters always want to hear the more spectacular, outrageous stories when they themselves wanted oftentimes to deal with more everyday concerns in their own lives such as problems in relationships, careers and parenting? People answered my question by telling me that if others could climb the mountain, then certainly they could climb the hill. "Inspire us!" "Tickle our fancy and imagination . . . for we do want to be happy." In addition, they suggested that through the veil of unhappiness, every hill looks like a mountain anyway.

Since we have been taught systematically to use unhappiness as emotional fuel (judging, fearing and pushing in order to take care of ourselves), seeking happiness first and happiness now truly makes any "be happy" adventurer an exception to the common rule. All my life, I heard about what I could not do or achieve and about how my dreams were unrealistic. When I compare the misery I used to feel with the happiness and love I experience today, I am awed. I never would have believed such a transformation could be possible.

When Samahria and I started working with our autistic son, our program to help him cure himself was condemned as silly, based on an impossible dream. I have witnessed, firsthand, many wonderful people making the impossible possible in their own lives. Nothing has moved me more than watching the birth of happiness and love and seeing the fruits that come from living in happiness and love. If we can bring that alive in our lives, then certainly nothing is impossible.

When any of us choose to prioritize happiness, we have made our journey an exceptional one. Not difficult, not lengthy, just unusual! We can turn the predictions of experts and the lessons of the past into rules and limitations, or we can choose to be the dreamers who bring our dreams to life.

Empowering ourselves to be happy and loving might be truly exceptional today. However, as we walk such a path, we pave the way for others who might one day find such an accomplishment commonplace.

The following thoughts, information and stories are meant to tickle and inspire us to change our beliefs, revise our world picture and take charge, more and more, of our power to choose happiness.

No one could have anticipated the immense impact the Industrial Revolution would have on the planet and all its inhabitants. A few hundred years of invention and production profoundly transformed landscapes and lifestyles which had previously evolved slowly over hundreds, thousands and even millions of years. Much of the magic burst forth from the insights of Isaac Newton, who uncovered reliable laws governing the movement of objects in space. He fashioned through his intricate mathematical computations a knowable, predictable and, therefore, conquerable world. Everything around us became comprehensible, better yet, useful or capable of being used. Order prevailed!

Then, suddenly, when this century was still so very young and new, revolutionary scientific theories such as those of relativity and quantum physics exploded into view. The upstarts of this new perspective claimed the universe to be neither reliable, absolutely predictable nor consistent. They delved into a subatomic inner space in which the tiniest particles, from electrons to quarks, followed paths sometimes haphazard and mystifying. At best, they suggested, we could make educated guesses about the nature of the evolving world. Events are probable, never certain! Out of this fledgling viewpoint came new technology producing lasers, microwaves, nuclear fission, fusion and the like. What a previous generation and culture had clutched as the final world view yielded to an even more insightful and powerful one. The science fiction fantasies of one century became the everyday mechanics of the next.

A neurologist in England specializes in examining and helping patients who are hydrocephalic as a result of birth defects, disease or trauma. Their brain cavities fill with cerebrospinal fluid that presses on and, in most cases, damages brain tissue, leaving these individuals seriously brain impaired and retarded. One day, this physician performed a brain scan on a gifted college student (I.Q. 126) with an enlarged cranium (a hydrocephalic indicator), although the young man had no medical history suggesting such a problem. To the amazement of this doctor and his staff, the scan revealed that this student had a mere microscopic layer of brain tissue one millimeter thick, with fluid in place of the complex network of the neurons required for thinking, remembering and speaking. In effect, a huge portion of his skull contained liquid instead of the normal brain tissue. Despite his lack of essential cerebral matter, this young man functioned at a high intellectual level in a highly competitive environment. Subsequently other physicians around the world have documented similar cases.

If this young person and others like him can function with great skill and talent without a complete brain, what can we do? If we are breathing, walking and talking, we are not only adequately equipped but probably overequipped with the power to choose happiness.

A professor at a major American university conducted an intriguing experiment with a binary random generator, designed to turn on and off in a random fashion but conforming with the laws of probability. This machine, despite its purposely inconsistent operation, will (over a period of hours and days) turn on about fifty percent of the time and turn off about fifty percent of the time. This conforms to what happens when a coin is flipped over a period of time; although random in occurrence, heads and tails will come up in approximately equal proportions.

Hooked to a heat lamp in a shed, the binary random generator operated in a way consistent with its design until, one day, the professor chose to shelter his cat from the cold by placing him in the shed. When he returned later, he noted to his surprise that during the cat's stay, the generator turned the lamp on noticeably more than half the time, violating its own mechanics. Once the professor removed his cat, the binary random generator resumed operating in the correct fifty/fifty fashion.

Much speculation ensued. Did the machine, which had no life in a way we comprehend, accommodate the cat in its desire to be warm? Or was the cat clairvoyant and telekenetic and thus able to control the machine's operation to achieve its own end? Or were both the cat and the machine somehow hooked into yet another dimension which understood the possibilities of the situation and effected what certainly appeared to be a "user-friendly" solution for the cat? Although machines are silicone-based and we (cat included), as living creatures, are formed from carbon-based molecules, could the electrons common to all matter resonate information simultaneously throughout the fabric of the universe in order to be helpful? Anything is possible!

A university cardiologist at a California hospital conducted a rather fanciful exploration. He did a computer-generated, double-blind experiment in remote healing. The study included 393 seriously ill cardiac patients. From this group, 192 were selected randomly for special treatment. They and their conditions were described in detail to people around the country who had been asked to pray for their health and recovery. Five to seven participants had been selected to pray daily for each one of these 192 patients and focus their prayers on the "beneficial healing and quick recovery" of the person identified. The remaining patients were given the usual quality medical care, but without the prayers.

Ten months later, the results of the experiment sparked the imagination of many. The people who had been prayed for (and did not know it) by others living at remote distances across the country experienced markedly fewer incidences of cardiac-related infections, pulmonary edema and mortality than did the 201 patients not included. As no visible hard wiring existed between the patients and the people praying for them, no one knew how to justify the undeniable results.

Oftentimes, phenomena resulting from experimentation remains unexplained, since much of science (the art of explanation) remains in its infancy. However, we can still be awed by people's good intentions and the power of their prayers. If we can accomplish so much at a distance, what might we achieve in the bodymind we inhabit? Have we prayed lately for the gift of happiness and love in our own lives and elsewhere on the planet? Nothing is impossible. We count! We can make a difference!

The bones in our bodies seem so solid and stable, unlike the everchanging measurements of our waist, thighs and buttocks. However, bones respond to stress by "growing" into whatever shape best matches the demands made on them. If we bend our leg consistently as part of an exercise or to operate machinery, the tissue on the stretched side of the bend will be reabsorbed in order to regrow and shore up the compressed side. Baseball players have heavier and differently contoured bones in their pitching arms than in their non-pitching arms. Tennis players have re-formed bone development which reinforces their racket arm. The process is one of actual regeneration. Cells from the sheath around the stretched side of the bone de-differentiate (transform themselves into more simple, embryolike cells), then migrate to the other side and differentiate (grow) into bone tissue.

Due to a clerical error in a hospital in England, doctors neglected to perform a closure on the end of a child's finger after the tip had been severed in an accident. When a surgeon finally arrived to do the procedure, she noticed to her surprise that a regeneration process had begun. Rather than interfere, she allowed the healing to continue. Within three months, the entire end of the finger had grown back without any deformity. From the hundreds of similar cases since documented, one common fact has emerged. Only young children experience regeneration; adolescents and adults, who do not believe people can regrow limbs, do not. Some hypothesize that the organization potential of cells might change as we age, thereby limiting possibilities. Others wonder about the power of our beliefs. Regeneration had been considered impossible before research became more sophisticated and before one surgeon capitalized on an error by allowing nature to run its course.

If we can regenerate tissue and even body parts (no one questions our ability to regrow part of our liver), then surely we can change beliefs and the neurology that supports them. If happiness were the seed, what bodymind would grow from it?

A family gathered in one of our meeting rooms at the Institute to begin the process of learning how to work directly with their special child using The Son-Rise Program^{SM} we teach. Hours had been spent questioning attitudes and expectations so that each person could develop, as best they could, a capacity to be present and unconditional in their interactions with this youngster. When we talked about bringing energy, enthusiasm and excitement to all contact, the parents looked sympathetically at the child's grandmother. This lady, who had recently celebrated her seventy-fourth birthday, had been restricted in her movements for several years because of a progressive case of arthritis. Her daughter tried gently to convince her to stand aside and not participate. But this woman, loving her grandchild passionately, claimed she would muster up the necessary energy and pleaded to be allowed to join the program. No one wanted to deny her that opportunity.

When her turn came to play with the child, she approached the room slowly, dragging her feet while holding her aching hips. She smiled at us self-consciously as she entered the room. What occurred in the next twenty minutes left every observer breathless. Slowly but surely, as she generated energy and enthusiasm in the teaching process, she moved more and more easily. Her joy in her special grandson could not be contained. By the middle of the session, this lady moved her arms and legs wildly as if she had been agile and aerobically well-exercised.

Later, after leaving the room and closing the door, she

slowed her walk abruptly and moved hesitantly toward the kitchen. The staff decided to observe without commentary. During the intervening time before her next session, this grandmother once again moved in a very restricted manner, obviously handicapped by her debilitating disease. However, once in the room again with the youngster, she came alive and the same ease and agility returned to all her movements.

In a feedback session that afternoon, we shared our observations with her. Although surprised, she acknowledged how different she had felt in the room. Why, she wondered, if she could be that way in the room, was she so different outside? Had her delight and happiness with her grandchild acted as a tonic, impacting on every joint in her body? She made a decision not to limit her love and acceptance to the confines of the room. Over the next few days, she not only turned, walked and sat down more easily outside of the playroom, but began to clown around and jostle others physically. The restrictive swelling ebbed and the pain eased noticeably.

We could probably analyze her body chemistry at the time she infused her bodymind with happiness and joy and doubtless uncover certain specific neuropeptides and neurotransmitters to explain her newly acquired physical dexterity. But we could not as easily quantify the power of her decision to reach out in happiness and love to her grandson and, in the process, transform her own life. Anything is possible—at any age!

———

At twenty-seven years old, Lorraine had become afraid to leave her house. Although talented, sophisticated and attractive, she hid from the world, scared to be far from home when one of her frequent panic attacks would envelop her. Therapists had labeled her problem with a fanciful term—agoraphobia.

She had endured endless physical examinations and had searched her body for any frailty which might result in her early demise. She focused her attention on her heart, fearing a life-threatening heart attack might be more probable if her heart rate increased. To protect herself, she not only monitored her pulse and blood pressure but also tried to make sure she did not walk too fast, speak too fast or climb stairs too fast. Although every noninvasive study revealed a strong and healthy heart, Lorraine dared not test those findings.

When this young woman came to spend the day with me, she requested tensely that our dialogue sessions be done sitting rather than walking, which had been my preference. We agreed to an easy compromise—slow walking.

The exploration of her agoraphobia hinged on her concern about her heart and her fear of death in a lonely, unforgiving place like an office, a department store or the sidewalk of a busy city street. Staying home insulated her from that possibility. Ultimately, she chose dying as the most pertinent issue to explore and identified concerns about the location of death as a secondary problem. Searching further, Lorraine found a belief which had been underlying this cycle of fear. She believed death to be final, with no possibility of additional experiences. In addition, and most polarizing for her, she envisioned herself transformed into useless dust. Therefore, only life as she now knew it had meaning and she had to protect each moment for living. When I asked her to define living, Lorraine laughed, then said, "Not what I am doing, certainly. Living is daring to be me. Living is enjoying our walk and my ability to think. Living is not being afraid of not living."

For the first time in hours, she laughed, wondering why she had not thought about all this before. Armed with her new vision of "living," she wanted to reconsider the "useless dust" idea. Within minutes, she decided, to her own amusement, that dust could be a medium of another dimension of life or simply perfect in its dustlike quality. "Dust could have a very special role in the universe," she declared with a smile. Lorraine had changed her vision.

As we continued the session, I noticed how she had increased the pace of our walking. She talked about how she used to jog but had not done so in years because of her fears.

"Would you want to try to jog now?" I asked.

Her mouth dropped open. She answered, "No," at first,

then converted her response slyly into a qualified "Yes." She contemplated an increase in her pulse rate, then agreed to run if I ran with her.

Like slow motion dancers, we began our run together with measured steps, continuing our dialogue as the wind whipped through our hair. Her pulse climbed to over one hundred, then to one hundred and twenty, then to one hundred and thirty-five. Lorraine began to laugh and cry at the same time. "I'm not dead!" she shouted. "I'm very much alive. And if I die now, what a wonderful last minute." She didn't die. She grabbed my hand firmly, insisted on running for another ten minutes and continued laughing and crying all the way.

Lorraine changed her life that day. Now no longer agoraphobic or panicked, she has become an exercise buff and resumed a career she had previously short-circuited. No vision of ourselves or the universe has been cast in cement. Whenever we want, in response to personal difficulties, we can reconsider our viewpoints and conclusions and change them. However, we do not require a problem as a stimulus to reorder priorities and make our daily living experience more of what we truly want. We can decide now! By changing our vision and our beliefs, we will dissolve the habits and/or phobias produced by them. Most important, we don't have to judge our illusions even as we try to change them.

———

Sometimes, when greeting a surprising turn of events or an unanticipated difficulty, I imagine a rather jolly and playful universe peering down at me and saying: "Okay, you think you have it together; well, my friend, try this challenge on for size." I could never accurately predict how I might deal with an upcoming dilemma, but I hope that my conviction about the value of happiness will continue to give me the strength and clarity to be, at the very least, loving and useful in the face of any circumstance. The following situation would have overwhelmed me years ago before I learned to live the empowering attitude of happiness, love and acceptance.

My oldest daughter leaned toward me, squeezing my hands tightly while pleading silently for help through the riveting gaze of her dark brown eyes. This episode of arrhythmia, one of hundreds, had continued now for almost thirty-three hours. Although she was sitting, her heart raced at almost one hundred and eighty beats a minute in a dizzying dance of changing rhythms and missed beats. Pain radiated from the center of her chest into her arms. Her fingers tingled with a fluctuating numbness. She panted, taking shallow breaths, fighting the sensation of suffocating to the point of exhaustion.

"I can't bear the thought of going to the hospital again," she whispered tearfully, "but I can't stand this anymore." She had held off, enduring sensations similar to those experienced during a heart attack while hoping this episode would pass. However, she acknowledged what the cardiologists had insisted, that once the wild rhythms begin, emergency room medical assistance provides the only real source of help. Yet such "corrections" of the arrhythmia were fleeting. Many times, hours after she endured the hospital trauma associated with rectifying the problem, the rhythm would break again, leaving her more exhausted than ever to face another devastating episode of runaway heartbeats. On occasion, medical intervention had created a heart block which has had dangerous, almost deadly, consequences.

I released one of my hands from the vise of my daughter's grip and stroked her face gently. I stayed present, loving her. Just two weeks before, we had celebrated her twentieth birthday. She had cried that night, wondering whether she would be able to complete her last year in college because of her escalating disability and whether she would live long enough to have a family, work with children and realize any other of her young dreams. We talked for hours as she tried to make sense out of her situation and use it to learn and grow. With the help of questions, she searched for her own answers and understanding. On rare occasions, she would laugh, deciding to be happy with the universe and her body anyway. But now, in the midst of this episode, she had lost some of her footing despite her valiant struggle to maintain bodily control.

"What do you think, Popi?" she asked. "Should I go to the hospital?"

"Do whatever you think is best. If you want to go to the hospital, that's fine," I said softly. We both knew emergency room intervention had its risks. Twice in the last eighteen months, her blood pressure plunged dangerously and the chambers of her heart malfunctioned as a result of the unpredictable side effects of intravenous medication administered on an emergency basis in a hospital. "We're sort of standing between a rock and a hard place. I could tell you what I think, Bryn, but maybe, what's more important is what you think. What do *you* want to do? Whatever you decide, I'll be there with you."

She pushed out a half smile. "I want to do it myself, Popi, but I can't. They said I can't." The cardiologists viewed her condition as congenital and believed the arrhythmia to be under the control of her autonomic nervous system. Thus, they theorized, no act of will could change the arrhythmia once it had begun. "Do I believe them?" she asked herself aloud. "Yes," she answered.

"Why do you believe them?" I questioned.

"Because I've never been able to do it myself."

"Okay, let's say in the past that's been true. Why does that mean you can't do it now?"

"It doesn't. It just means I couldn't do it yesterday. I guess I could try again, but I've tried so many times before."

She shook her head. "This will never work unless I really think I can do it."

"Can you?" I asked.

"I want to believe I can. There I go again, doubting myself rather than being happy and trusting me." She stopped speaking, struggling to pull in enough air. "Okay. I can. I will. I guess I'll get the stethoscope."

She giggled for the first time in two days as she adjusted the instrument in her ears and placed the listening cup over her heart. I held her hands as she closed her eyes and concentrated. Ten seconds passed; then twenty, then a minute. Her eyes opened limply. "It's still going wild. Nothing's changing."

"Bryn, as you listen, what are you thinking?"

She sighed. "How one wild beat follows another. Even when it beats regularly for one or two beats, I kind of listen for the next series of crazy beats."

Suddenly, she realized she had conditioned herself to always anticipate the arrhythmias rather than to visualize a smooth, regular rhythm. "Maybe I could wait for the next regular beat, anticipate the next regular beat and then visualize one regular beat followed by another." She sighed noisily. "Okay, I'm going to try that."

She nodded, closed her eyes and continued to monitor her heartbeats. Her hands gripped mine tightly, then abruptly began to quiver. A funny gurgling sound came from her throat. I held my breath, staring at her, not knowing what was happening. The quivering increased and increased, but her face appeared paradoxically serene. Then, quite suddenly, she opened her eyes as an avalanche of tears cascaded down her face. "I did it. Oh my God, I did it."

She placed the stethoscope in my ears. What I heard was the most amazing music . . . a steady, even rhythm of heart-beats.

For Bryn, this event would be one victory among many more to come as she dared to challenge the seemingly impossible; for me, it offered opportunities to make my love and support for her tangible and, hopefully, useful . . . one day at a time.

I think not of "what if," but of "what is." And so, each day, I celebrate her continuing life and her passion to live so fully.

People never anticipate their children dying; they bury such thoughts in the dark recesses of their minds. But for Ted and his wife, Allison, their worst nightmare became a reality.

All three of their children were lively little people—healthy, curious, busy and a bit mischievous. But Brian, the youngest, had a special aptitude for charming adults with his little boy insights and easy displays of affection. His colorful cartoons and drawings decorated his parents' and grandparents' homes. His enthusiasm, questions and commentaries beguiled family and friends alike.

One day his grandmother asked him what he wanted for his next birthday, which was months away. "Oh," Brian said, "it doesn't matter, Grandma. I won't be here by my next birthday." The grandmother, startled by the comment, chose not to probe the little boy for more information. A week later, Brian gave his grandmother an ambitious drawing of his family, saying, "This is how much I love you. You can keep it so you can always remember how much I love you, even when I'm not here." Once again the grandmother listened with curiosity, but did not question the meaning underlying her grandchild's comment.

On a Saturday, a few weeks before his birthday, Brian accompanied his father while he ran errands. Normally, Brian delighted in shopping and talking to people in stores, and Ted loved having him with him. However, on this day, this cute four-year-old complained about being tired and whined continuously. His father asked him to be patient and reminded him that he had volunteered to come. Resisting his father's requests, Brian asked to go home. Ted declared that he would have to wait until he finished his chores and scolded his son more than once.

After arriving home, he noticed that his bouncy little youngster, who rarely got sick, had a mild fever. When Brian himself suggested resting, his father tucked him in bed, feeling somewhat guilty about his earlier impatience now that he saw his son had apparently been coping with a cold or the flu. Several hours later, Brian's fever increased. Ted and Allison tried to reach their family physician. By the time he returned their phone call, Brian's fever had climbed even higher. Wishing to err on the side of caution, they agreed to meet the doctor at the hospital so he could examine him more completely.

Two hours later, Brian smiled at his parents and closed his eyes as he had done hundreds of times in their presence. But this time, within a few hours, Brian died. His parents' screams of shock and agony rippled through the corridor of the hospital. Death had come unannounced and stolen their son on a day marked by the most ordinary of circumstances. No warning! No preparation! No chance even to say good-bye.

Ted and Allison clung to their child's body, hoping their love and caring would somehow magically bring him back. But, as he had predicted, Brian would not be there for his next birthday celebration. Later, his aunt discovered that the complex drawing that Brian had given his grandmother depicted all the members of his family with one exception—Brian.

Within twenty-four hours, we received a call from the grandmother who, like Ted and Allison, had come from Canada and attended several of our programs. She asked if we could work with the entire family and help them assimilate their horror in the face of this event. The next evening, Brian's parents, grandparents, aunts and uncles and cousins arrived at our Institute. We gathered together, seating ourselves in a giant circle. Everyone had visual contact with each other in the room. I asked all those present to express their feelings and thoughts in turn, as well as share what they wanted most for themselves during our time together.

Allison talked about how she may have failed Brian. Somehow, as his mother, she should have known what even the doctors did not know. If she had acted sooner, maybe she could have saved her baby. Ted tried to make sense out of his behavior toward Brian during his last day of life. He had loved him more than anyone could imagine, and yet he would forever see in his mind Brian's last hours contaminated by his impatience. The possibility of losing Brian, his only son, or either of his daughters had been his worst fear—a fear he believed every parent harbored. Why had the worst event imaginable happened to him and to this sweet little person?

Brian's grandmother kept reviewing conversations she had had with this spunky child. Had Brian known about his own death in some way? Why hadn't she pursued what now seemed like messages from this little boy? The grandfather sat stoically for a long time before sharing his thoughts and feelings; then he raised his eyes upward and pointed toward the heavens. "What kind of God would do this?" he asked.

He wanted an explanation, though he believed none would ever be forthcoming.

Brian's uncle began to cry as he spoke. "When I went home from the hospital, I couldn't believe Brian had died. He was so alive two days ago, so healthy. I really loved that kid. When I got home, I kept thinking about my daughter Deidre and how she could just disappear that easily. You know what I did? I climbed into bed with her and just kept watching her to make sure that she was breathing. I think I slept less than an hour the whole night. I thought that if I kept watching her, I could keep her safe. I was so afraid I'd lose her like Ted and Allison and all of us have lost Brian."

An aunt shared that she wanted to be of some comfort to Ted and Allison during this terrible time but felt ill-equipped. Brian's ten-year-old cousin talked about missing her little friend and wondered who would take care of him now. Tears punctuated her words. Hours passed during that initial sharing, allowing each person the time and space to open themselves to their feelings and thoughts and join with others in trying to understand what had just happened to all of them.

Allison thanked everyone in the room for loving her son so sincerely. Holding her husband's hand tightly, she asked me to ask her questions. She wanted to move through her sense of failure so she could stop focusing on herself and remember Brian more clearly. In the process of dialoguing with me, Allison came to realize that she had done the best she could for Brian and decided that Brian would know.

Ted agreed with his wife and, in that instant, decided to forgive himself. Even through his impatience with his son on the day of his death, he had communicated his love to him in endless ways. He had given him a piggyback ride in one store, played a tickling game with him in the car and sat with him in his bedroom until he fell asleep. Like Allison, he knew Brian would have felt his love and caring. Resolving these concerns, he then turned his attention to what he called the nightmare of losing him. "Why, when you have something in your life so precious, do you always worry about losing it?" he asked. His answer bubbled to the surface quickly. "Because," he said, "I couldn't imagine living without him. But, you know," he added, "I'm not living without him." He pounded his chest. "He's here. He will always be here. As long as I'm alive, he will be alive." Tearful smiles from those in the circle greeted this father's declaration. They, too, would keep him close.

The grandmother reviewed again her unwillingness to question Brian's pronouncements and recalled that when she herself had been a child, she used to have premonitions like her own grandson's. Sometimes her thoughts scared her. Rather than deal with intuitions she believed herself incapable of handling, she blotted them out of her awareness as she had done with Brian's inexplicable remarks. She continued to speak, recalling with pinpointed detail another incident in which Brian had talked about "going away" sometime soon. Never did this child seem troubled or frightened by such a possibility. His grandmother had never catalogued that realization before. Even Brian's death had been a gentle experience; the little boy had died peacefully. In that moment, Brian's grandmother began to smile broadly. "I didn't know what to do with his premonitions, but I think he did."

The grandfather protested this conclusion. He wanted God pulled onto the carpet. "Such bright eyes. Such laughter. Such love. It's just not fair. He had no right to take him!" However, once he acknowledged that he could not pretend to understand God's motivation, he switched to a more personal grievance. Brian had been cheated out of the possibility of a long and happy life, and he had been deprived of being part of it. Brian had had a particular fondness for his grandfather and, frequently, cuddled up in his lap with such delight. The older man had enjoyed his grandson tremendously, though he had never really shared with him just how much he adored him. Oh yes, he could talk about this affectionate youngster to his colleagues and friends, but why, he wondered, had he never told Brian directly how much he meant to him?

Ted gaped at his father in amazement. "That's your style, Dad. You never express appreciation."

The older man leaned forward sternly. Another one of his

sons in the circle supported Ted's statement. Removing his glasses and blinking in surprise, this man looked at his grown boys, who worked with him daily in the family's construction business, and shook his head. "I tell you!"

"No, you don't," Ted countered. "You tell us what we've done wrong and what you want us to do better. You never say you appreciate our input. You never thank us. You just expect a certain level of performance and, if we don't produce, you cut us down. Really, Dad, that's the way it is!"

No one spoke as Brian's grandfather searched the faces in the circle, silently soliciting support. Slowly and reluctantly, he opened himself to the truth of his son's evaluation. He reached his hand out toward Ted. "May I tell you now?" the man whispered in the most gentle way, as he wiped tears from his face. Ted nodded.

"I could never have done the business without you. You and each of your brothers, well, have made it all work for me. When I see you fellows each morning, I feel proud and I feel blessed to have such sons, to be able to work with you. Proud and blessed. I appreciate your hard work. I do." He continued sharing similar feelings with each of his boys while everyone listened and watched in amazement.

When he finished speaking, Allison looked around at the members of her family and said, "Brian gave this to all of us." Then she turned to her father-in-law and smiled. "Papa, to see you like this, well, I never thought . . ."

The family patriarch put his face in his hands and, uncharacteristically, sobbed in the presence of others. No one moved until Ted reached out to embrace his father in a rare hug; then the others gathered close to share their affection.

Brian's death had become a healing. Although no one could explain the meanderings of the river, with its unexpected twists and turns, this family found beauty and love in what others might have experienced as an intolerable misfortune. They had turned a tragedy into a gift. Through the late hours of the night and beginning again the next morning, these people confronted their innermost concerns and shared fears and secrets never before verbalized. Brian's name was upon everyone's lips, and his life had become an inspiration to be open and honest and honoring of each other as he had been with each of them during his brief life.

We had spent one short day together. When the family left, a sense of exuberance bonded them. Their smiles, as well as their peaceful and, yes, happy faces, stood in marked contrast to the somber, pained glances around the circle during those first hours. They had given Brian's life so much power and significance by the way they chose to respond to his death.

In the darkness we can find light. In the confusion of seemingly senseless events, we can find meaning. In the ab-

sence of a dear one, we can continue to find happiness, love and peace of mind. We are the belief-makers. Our ability to design and influence personal and shared experiences knows no bounds. In such a user-friendly universe, nothing is impossible.

VI · Shortcuts to Happiness

IMPLEMENTING THE
HAPPINESS OPTION

Dear Sweet Readers: If you have jumped to this chapter in the book, wonderful! However, after reading whatever sections you want, I would like to encourage you to backtrack to the beginning of the book and read the other chapters which I believe will create a strong foundation from which you can then easily implement the life-changing suggestions presented here.

LOVE, BEARS

To live consciously and to root our actions in clear intentions neither compromises spontaneity nor diminishes the unfolding miracle of who we are. We can engineer our own responses, choosing love over hate, peace over conflict and happiness over depression. In making those choices, we seed and then nurture the human landscape with distinctly tender and joyful hands. Shortcuts to happiness then become short-cuts to peace, cooperation, communion and love.

These tools for taking charge, which fit so naturally and easily into our hands, allow us to replace discipline with celebration and substitute years of questionable study and therapeutic soul-searching with simple reminders. We are all fully equipped; we have only to exercise our winning option—our shortcuts to happiness.

Where do these shortcuts originate? Thousands of people have come our way in their pursuit of happiness. Some have faced external circumstances that challenged their fortitude and emotional stability. Others negotiated with internal demons and judgments which sabotaged relationships, careers and other potentially life-affirming experiences. Still others fenced expertly with doubts and confusion, keeping happiness at bay until they had all the answers (which, of course, they never did).

So many of us cling stubbornly to our miseries and, at times, even resist all attempts to remove them. We charge the walls of unhappiness like courageous crusaders, staunchly defending our words and deeds even while we want to let go of them. We act as if it matters to make sense out of how we have behaved. We want to move forward, but our feet drag in the quicksand of our own judgments. We become exhausted by the process and create impasses for ourselves.

In our work with individuals and groups, we have witnessed such impasses dissolving in the face of acceptance. When we greet people's discomforts and self-incrimination with an attitude of love and acceptance, they tend to relax their guard and begin the process of unearthing the beliefs which have fueled their unhappiness. Their struggle becomes a dance. Judgments melt away. They become more self-trusting and more self-accepting. They develop a sense of inner peace. They realize that they are not against themselves in spite of self-defeating behavior. In fact, they always do the best they can and act with the best of intentions.

Over the passing years, Samahria and I, as well as others who live and teach at The Option Institute and Fellowship, have had increasing opportunities to observe and interact with people who have made moving vigorously toward happiness a conscious intention and a central focus in their lives. Some time ago, we began to notice in such people, as well as ourselves, definite qualities or character traits that we concluded happier people seem to share and maximize. As we analyzed these traits, we wondered whether or not they, in themselves, constituted pathways to happiness. When people choose deliberately to be happier and more loving, do they, in addition, discover insights and teach themselves tricks to facilitate and sustain their journey? Absolutely!

As these attitudinal pioneers had been our students, we

now became theirs. We wanted to catalogue their collective wisdom and choices so that their sincere pursuit of happiness would yield shortcuts for those who followed. We loved the process of nonjudgmental exploration; we watched with awe the transformations it wrought. However, we loved happiness even more. As we watched some people dialogue endlessly with great fascination but limited results while others used the dialogue process to make huge leaps toward happiness, we wondered, how could we facilitate an easier, more immediate change for everyone?

Initially, we itemized over thirty-two separate perspectives to study. As we delved deeper, a number of these different pathways to happiness merged into one another until we could distinguish fifteen. Finally, as we became more astute anthropologists of beliefs and behavior, the fifteen paths merged even further until reduced to six key shortcuts to happiness. Although we could see each as distinct, we knew immediately that all six shortcuts were merely six facets of one decision: *the decision to be happy*! Nevertheless, distinguishing varied shortcuts allowed us to make the experience of happiness more accessible, easy and instantaneous.

The "decision to be happy" is actually the decision to stop being unhappy.

We came into the world fully equipped to be happy and then became systematically educated to be unhappy and use unhappiness as a tool of growth, manipulation and camaraderie. We did what we believed would be best to take care of ourselves, but now we can create concrete opportunities to choose differently. We can claim our birthright and yield to the yearning inside. Every shortcut, by enabling us to pull the plug quickly and easily on discomfort, maximizes our power to experience happiness (the feeling we enjoy when we are not being unhappy).

We observed that when people took just one of the six shortcuts, their lives changed immediately. When they took two or more, the shift appeared even more dramatic, globally transforming their responses. How awesome to witness the clarity and ingenuity of those dedicated to living their lives more happily and what a gift to share the same self-empowering options with others!

We knew, however, that these shortcuts in themselves could not help us to be happier unless we converted them into concrete action with sincere and abiding energy and enthusiasm. The insights come alive when we apply them to specific situations and use them to embrace ourselves as well as the people and events of our lives.

We can choose to live the dream of love and happiness instead of just dreaming it. The roadway lies before us. We need only to take one easy step at a time.

Creating the Happiness Arc.

Although the study of the brain and the bodymind connections remains in its infancy, little pearls of information have already revolutionized our understanding of thinking and the physical components of thought. Years ago, researchers demonstrated that the neurons in our brains not only never grow but also actually decline in number with age. They concluded the brain descends slowly, day by day, into a state of dysfunction, which might include memory loss, impaired ability to think logically, even senility. They saw the race against time as leaving us all mentally diminished.

However, more sophisticated data now clearly illustrate that although millions of neurons do, indeed, disappear each year, the dendrites or arms of remaining neurons have an amazing capacity to branch, stretch, extend and grow when stimulated. This capacity increases our ability to reason and to retain information faster than the loss of neurons decreases it. In addition, the glial cells, which lie between the dendrites and which secrete chemicals that support neural transmissions, also proliferate when stimulated. Rather than shrinking with age, a stimulated and exercised mind will expand physically and become heavier through use. As we can "body build" we can "mind build" as well.

The manner and content of our thinking creates the software of the bodymind. Unlike computer software, however, the software of the bodymind generates new hardware. In effect, our thoughts can cause our brains to grow. More than ever before, we realize that the beliefs with which we fill our brains not only become bodywide neurotransmitters and neuropeptides capable of communicating instantly with the fifty trillion cells in our body but also impact on the growth and density of our dendrites.

Imagine dendrites as billions of little fingers in our brain. With repetitive thoughts and actions, we have trained these fingers to form particular patterns or arcs, which become well traveled neurological roadways. Unhappiness might be one of many roadways we have created with our thoughts and actions. Therefore, we might be able to conclude that we would more likely respond with anger, impatience, jealousy or fear if we have grown or "programmed" our dendrites with thoughts or "software" leading to such feelings.

Choosing happiness constitutes a profoundly different alternative in this flexible, user-friendly internal universe, allowing us to redesign the landscape. Each time we choose peace, acceptance, forgiveness and love, we make it possible for our neural fingers to develop a new configuration which I call metaphorically the "Happiness Arc." The more we make such choices, the larger and stronger the arc becomes, until happiness begins to evolve as the more commonplace and more accessible experience. As we might seem likely now to react to an insult with anger, to rejection with sadness and to criticism with defensiveness, so comfort, inner peace and joy might easily become more "natural" responses as we choose happiness and love over and over again.

Since the aim of this sharing is not to fill our cups as if they were empty, but to bring what we know more acutely alive, the following will probably appear somewhat obvious and familiar. How wonderful! Take this familiarity as a reassuring sign. Our communion with the shortcuts enables us to activate them very easily in our lives. Frequently, we search laboriously for complex, remote solutions when the simplest and most obvious ones, which we may have overlooked, can facilitate the most significant personal miracles.

We can take the shortcuts now and claim our birthright to happiness. Our choices will become our destiny. Our many choices to be happy (accessible in an instant by virtue of a decision) will create life-affirming and life-sustaining happiness arcs.

Shortcut # 1—Make Happiness The *Priority!*

Happiness first! Happiness now! Just bringing happiness (and love) to the center of the stage will make a profound difference. Although the validity of this statement might appear obvious, rarely do we put happiness first in our lives.

An elementary school teacher shared with us a revealing survey she had conducted among her third grade pupils. She had asked them to itemize a list of "wants." In response, a vast variety of preferences surfaced. The pupils put trips to the amusement park, the latest Lego set, space travel, dolls that talked, a new bicycle, longer gym periods, no more homework and a fanciful array of video games on their lists. Nowhere on their papers did the children include the "want" to be happy or more loving.

Certainly our schools and universities do not include the pursuit of happiness in their curricula (no Happiness 101 offered along with Algebra 101). If we look at course offerings as a reflection of our culture's concerns and values, we must conclude that being happy has not achieved even minimal recognition. And what kind of role models have our parents been for us or we for our children? Was being happy and loving ever said to be as significant as (or perhaps more significant than) being neat, getting good grades or abiding by the rules?

Fascinated by the results of the elementary school class

study, we conducted further surveys, including one with high school students. They wanted to be popular, to have a boyfriend or girlfriend, to excel in sports, to get a driver's license, to have longer vacations, to have attractive clothes and to get into a good college. One student said she wanted an exciting life. Another indicated he wanted to "time-travel." A similar questionnaire distributed to college students revealed desires to have a car (any car, as long as it had wheels), to have sex or more sex, to get good grades, to have less course work and more friends. Again, no stated desire to be happy. To be loved or loving never appeared anywhere.

A group in their middle twenties indicated new wants at the top of their lists. A meaningful relationship, a better job, more money and a comfortable apartment headed their concerns. Further down their lists we did note a different classification of preferences: "an easier life," "fewer hassles" and "more challenges." Those in their forties focused on still other concerns and issues: they wanted better relationships with their spouses, more respectful children, increased job opportunities as well as more financial security, less stress and more personal time. The wants presented by people in their sixties revealed new priorities: health, security, respect from others and a meaningful role in their community. Sporadically, words like "peace," "comfort" and even "happiness" appeared.

When we asked some of the list makers why they wanted

a new bicycle or a driver's license or a better job or more respect from their children or improved health, they indicated always that those events or items would make them happy. They sought happiness as the end product of all their wants and striving, yet had failed to mention directly this critical concern which underlay all others.

If we work so hard to make money, to have a relationship and to beautify our bodies because we believe any one of those accomplishments (or others we might itemize) would bring us happiness, we are clearly pointing to the ultimate feeling or experience we seek. Why then put mountains in our way?

"Love me more passionately," an older man pleads to his wife of thirty-three years. Why? Because it will make him happy, he answers. In fact, without it, he'll be unhappy (he promises her and himself). Thus unhappiness becomes the threat or motivator and happiness the end-goal (after passion).

A young mother, juggling a career and household responsibilities, asks her husband and children to acknowledge her contributions. Why? "Because," she replies, "the recognition will help me feel valuable and appreciated." Why does she want to feel valued and appreciated? Because she knows it will make her feel good (make her happy). However, appreciation does not "make" us happy. We give ourselves doses of "good feelings" in response to gratitude. Ironically, in contrast, some of us give ourselves doses of discomfort or even want to hide when others express gratitude directly to us. We design the game and the responses (which vary from person to person), then live it as if we are innocent bystanders. No indictments here! Just an opportunity! We have been systematically educated to buy a complex system of beliefs. We do the best we can based on those beliefs. Nevertheless, we can review them here and now . . . and change them if we choose!

A business executive ignores workaholic stress and demands increased production output from himself and other employees to improve the "bottom line." Why does he want greater profits since his company is already profitable? He believes such an accomplishment would bolster his financial security and investment equity. When asked why he wanted a larger nest egg, he stated that he could then finally relax and feel comfortable (happy) about any future contingency. Relaxation and comfort (aspects of happiness) had been the ultimate goal which he either withheld or made conditional upon reaching his personal "bottom line."

How wonderful to pursue passion, vitality and enthusiasm in our love relationships! How sweet, sensible and useful for any of us to encourage appreciation for our contributions (that would be a gift for both the giver and the receiver)! How challenging and exciting to produce more in the marketplace and enhance our own net worth at the same time! But why make our happiness (feeling good *inside*) dependent upon achieving those goals? Why not be happy now and then pursue whatever we want?

Years ago, I had a discussion with a neighbor who pointed to my life at that time as an example of good luck and good fortune. He talked about the publication of my latest book, the airing of a network television movie based on an earlier book, *Son-Rise*, our adoption of another child and the growing community of people seeking our service. In comparison, nothing happened for him that year. He would have been so happy, he said, had he resolved some of the many continuing disagreements he had had with his oldest daughter. He wanted a closer relationship with her, but since she had moved to another city, he reasoned there was little he could do, so he did nothing. He had hoped to find another job this year. However, he reported the job market in his profession had contracted due to the economy, so he decided it would be nonsensical to pursue a new position at this time. He expressed further concern that he might be viewed as less valuable since he had just celebrated his fiftieth birthday. He could not bear the thought of being rejected because of his age. Rather than face the loss of good feelings or the possibility of future discomfort, he extinguished his "wants" even before they became full-bodied. He never allowed himself to convert his thoughts and desires into action.

In response to his commentary, I suggested an alternative viewpoint. Did he know, for example, that I had wanted and pursued actively at least one hundred different items or events this year, some of which he might even deem nonsensical? Did he realize that the examples he catalogued about my life represented only four wants fulfilled in a hundred? In fact, as many as ninety-six of my other wants were never realized this year.

Since I choose not to tie my happiness to my getting these (therefore, I am not unhappy if I don't get what I want), then I am free, free to want and pursue anything—and everything! So what he envisioned as "good luck" had actually been a combination of my energy and the universe assisting me in manifesting about five percent of what I wanted. For those gifts, I feel truly grateful and blessed.

Often, we transform what we want into "a need to get" in order to be happy. We "need" the love, the recognition and the praise in order to feel good. As a result, our pursuits become distracted and burdened by fear of failure (if we don't get it, we will judge ourselves and be unhappy). Suppose we break the connection. Suppose we decide to prioritize happiness now and do all we can to be happy now, then pursue our goals. Rather than experience any loss in personal power, we would find ourselves far more energetic, creative and daring in striving for what we wanted since our happiness would no longer be at stake!

We develop our own series of personal prerequisites ("when people treat me respectfully," "when I have more money," "when I lose fifteen pounds") before allowing the real reward we have pursued. We hang happiness in front of us like the carrot before the donkey. Why couldn't we acknowledge the feeling we want to experience (or reclaim) and put it within our grasp at the very top of our "want" list? By thinking "happiness first, happiness now," we would be merely adjusting our priorities to more accurately reflect our primary pursuit.

One of my staff members once became very impatient with her assistant and talked angrily to her in order to motivate her to change. When I asked whether she wanted "change" more than happiness, she replied, "Let me get the office to run smoothly; then I'll be happy." Suddenly her mouth dropped open as she reviewed her own statement. "Wow!" she exclaimed. "Why would I do that?" What a different experience she created for herself when she selected happiness as her first priority and then, in an easy, direct, yet supportive manner, encouraged her assistant to change. Even if the anger appears to work (for the moment), do we want to fill our bodies with that sensation, with all its neurological and chemical components, rather than making inner peace with its bodily relaxation and comfort the focus of attention?

In dialogue sessions with couples, many times I hear one partner tell the other that what she (or he) really wants for herself (or himself) and the other person is happiness. After breaching the walls of judgment and silence, parents in our family programs indicate repeatedly the same simple want for their children to be happy. Yet, on the basis of their behavior just prior to that declaration, I would never have guessed a desire for happiness and love lay beneath the surface of family discord. Although many of us might have placed happiness on our list of wants, have we prioritized it?

Sometimes parents actually daydream about strangling their offspring, not as a serious gesture but as a fanciful form of appeasing their own anger or disappointment. Sally spent years trying to motivate her son to be more diligent with his schoolwork and more motivated in areas of personal hygiene. The more she struggled, trying to force him to adopt her values, the more he resisted. She felt she cared so intensely that fury could be her only reasonable response. Being comfortable or happy with her son meant giving up and losing the battle to reform him. Her son's actions had to change before she could breathe easy and develop a sense of inner peace and well-being.

After attending one of my talks, Sally gave herself permission to reconsider this perspective and flirt with the idea of making happiness *the* priority in her life. The next time her son delivered a note from school detailing his incomplete homework assignments, Sally experimented with this new intention and found she could be, by decision, remarkably at ease with the situation. In addition, she did not "give up" as she had anticipated she might, but became more decisive than usual in withdrawing certain privileges until he remedied the situation. When her son yelled his protest, Sally smiled at him, told him she no longer wanted to be the recipient of such verbal abuse and left the room without further commentary. She didn't hate him or herself, a reaction she had often had after one of their infamous altercations. She had prioritized happiness and, rather than compromising her parenting skills by such a choice, she experienced herself as more in charge and, ironically, more loving in her response.

Sally wrote me several letters detailing her many decisions to choose comfort and relinquish discomfort as the only reasonable reaction to her youngster's behaviors. "My son no longer has control over my unhappiness and happiness buttons . . . only I do." Sally described how the simple idea of choosing "happiness now" had become the facilitating mechanism underlying her growing "declaration of emotional independence."

A colleague shared with me a story about how making happiness a priority had profound impact for him while engaged in a lengthy argument with his wife. He had spent at least thirty minutes locked in a heated debate about how to spend family time during an upcoming weekend. He had wanted to refurbish an old table saw and then begin building a sun deck behind his home. His wife thought both of them should devote the day to shopping for window curtains before the sun bleached their newly-installed dark blue carpets. In the midst of battle, he realized that "winning" had become the sole focus of his attention. Then he recalled the notion of making happiness the priority. He resisted altering his position at first, feeling awesomely invested in the outcome of this quarrel. But finally, his inner dialogue dominated and he switched his driving force from focusing on getting his way to putting energy into trying to be accepting and loving. "Most of all," he reminded himself silently, "I want to be happy."

He stopped speaking mid-sentence, took a very deep breath and then declared, "There is nothing you can say to me that would diminish my love and good feelings for you. Whatever happens, I want us to be happy." A few moments of awkward silence ensued.

"Just a minute, buster, I know exactly what you're doing," his wife snapped. "I wasn't born yesterday. You're just trying to manipulate me so I will go along with you. Not a chance!"

"Although I still don't want to go shopping, more important to me is to be in touch with being happy and loving with you." He leaned across the table to kiss her, but she moved away swiftly. Again, deep inside, he reaffirmed his commitment to be happy and loving above all else. His wife protested this new development for at least ten minutes, but then, in the face of his consistently sweeter participation, she threw up her arms and laughed at his antics. They resolved their differences by deciding to spend half a day puttering at home and the other half shopping. But most significantly, this man reported how comfortable and relaxed he felt immediately following his decision to change his intention during the interaction.

A lawyer who attended one of our programs told us that prioritizing happiness precipitated a turning point in her legal practice. After days of reviewing depositions with her clients, she led them into court where they would litigate an action for nonpayment of bills. Everyone in her party seemed nervous. Suddenly, she surprised herself by blurting, "Let's remember that we want to present a strong case, but even more important we want to give ourselves a happy experience." Her clients gaped at her for a few speechless seconds, then followed her through the doors. Later, one of the men she represented told her that her comment had had an unexpected impact on him. Immediately after she made her statement, he relaxed his shoulders and eased his fistlike grip on his attaché case. During the entire courtroom process, he considered and reconsidered her novel suggestion and found himself surprisingly unmoved even in the face of misinformation presented by the opponents. He believed his ability to respond clearly to questions had been greatly enhanced by his decision to make the experience as pleasant as possible for himself. It never occurred to him that focusing on being comfortable would give him such an attitudinal advantage.

He out-performed himself in ways he would have never anticipated.

Admittedly, not all of her clients reacted the way this
man did. However, since that event, this attorney always
reminds her clients to give themselves, as best they can, a
comfortable, happy and internally peaceful experience even
while involved in divorce proceedings, child custody disputes
and complex business litigations. She reports a surprising
number of people actually act on her suggestion and new
referrals seek her counsel because of her growing reputation
as a lawyer who makes happiness part of the legal experience.

When we put energy into a relationship, a career or a
child, our desire is to create a situation with which we can be
happy. However, we tend to spend most of our days manipu-
lating the external environment while waiting for eventual
happiness rather than experiencing happiness now as a first
priority.

Without question, this becomes the most obvious shortcut. No place to go. No mountains to climb. No success to
achieve. No material items to acquire. We can pursue all our
goals from a happy place and not wait for external events to
materialize so we can be happy.

No reason to make happiness the dessert on the menu;
it can be the whole meal. Next time a lover talks angrily, a
coworker criticizes, a child screams or a parent scolds, we can
use that event to remind ourselves that first and foremost we

want to be happy. In effect, we decide not to push any unhappiness or misery buttons. We have the power to make that choice. Even in the face of an attack or a treasure lost, we can affirm our first priority in every situation—to be happy.

We can trust that our happiness will realign not only the dendrites in our brain but also the molecules of our material world and become a lullaby that will charm the universe.

Shortcut # 2—Personal Authenticity

In the early days of our teaching, some people raised the specter of the "happy idiot," expressing fear that, if people became happier and more loving, then the distinctive colors and shades of humanity would fade and blend, creating a dull, monochromatic canvas. We have noted just the opposite. As individuals become more comfortable and at ease (accepting and trusting of themselves and others), they tend to be more distinctly themselves. Thus, happiness accents rather than diminishes individuality. In fact, the happier person delights in her own idiosyncratic ways and uses personal authenticity as yet another useful tool to invite and support happiness.

Innocence often charms and inspires us. At a conference on healing in which I presented our work, I remember with excitement watching the austere demeanor of an upper-management executive dissolve as he cuddled a three-month-old infant in his arms during an intermission. Suddenly his face became animated; he cooed, clucked and smiled broadly. For a fleeting moment, the man lowered his mask and allowed his clownlike inner joy to surface. However, when he realized he had an admiring audience, he became self-conscious, returned the baby to its mother and resumed his more "serious" business manner. The innocence of a child had inspired an innocent and authentic response. This one adult had relaxed and met the child as a child. What would the impact be if we all began greeting the circumstances of our life like welcoming children?

A baby explores his world with dancing eyes. His tiny hands cup alien objects within the folds of newly wrinkled skin. Everything goes into his mouth as he uses his lips, tongue and gums to make contact with his external environment. No object in view escapes his curiosity and investigation. Even the most minute items, like the button on a shirt or a piece of lint on a carpet, become objects of delight. As a toddler, he pushes his little fingers into every hole, fondles everything he can touch and flies from one item to the next. He celebrates his humanity through his spontaneity, curiosity and delight. A diamond ring and a twisted nail hold the same fascination. Little people are forever busy, their endless motion unencumbered by judgments and self-incriminations. They are the planet's great adventurers, genuine explorers who dare to bring themselves fully to every experience. They don't simply go with their own flow; they are their own flow. They don't simply act happily; they are happiness in action.

Very young children are forever authentically themselves; they do not experience the internal dissonance and short circuits of role-playing in accordance with external standards. They take their cues from within. We recognize their innocence immediately as a precious commodity. Their uncensored presentness beguiles and intrigues us and, perhaps, becomes one of the major reasons we want to help and protect them.

One evening, when several guests entered our home, some of our children joined in greeting them. One of my sons, five years old at that time, said his sweet "hello" to one guest and then followed immediately with a question, "Why do you have such a big nose?"

Our visitor appeared momentarily startled, as did some of the others in the room. Then he laughed more robustly than I had ever seen him do before. He knelt down and took my son's hands. Still smiling brightly, he said, "You see how big I am. Very tall! Well, God gave me this big, big nose in front of my face so I wouldn't fall backwards. It helps me balance. What do you think? Do you like it?" My son reached forward, stroked the length of our guest's nose and nodded affirmatively. Everyone laughed.

When a child goes from person to person or activity to activity, the same little creature presents himself or herself in each circumstance. No protective masks are used, no roles modeled and no extra clothing worn to camouflage or impress others. Children naturally display a wholeness of person without study or premeditation. Most of us view those first years as sacred and blessed. And yet they do not endure. Rather than encourage such innocence, delight and enthusiasm, we quickly introduce cultural standards for everyone to follow.

Perhaps, in our childhood, our parents or guardians may have celebrated us for precious weeks, months or even years. They may have encouraged us to explore our fantasies and develop our imagination in a world of playful exploration. But then, inevitably, the agenda changed. For our own protection, those around us said we had to learn how to act, what to say and what to want. We became little belief consumers, internalizing notions of good and bad, right and wrong, should and should not. No one distinguished between prejudice and objective data. No one separated myths from facts. We internalized it all, mostly without question.

I remember emerging startled from a Sunday school class as a seven-year-old. That very morning the teacher had taught us the Ten Commandments, which, she explained, were rules from God that we had to obey. Thou shalt not kill! Thou shalt not steal! Until that lesson, it had never occurred to me that I might kill or steal or fail to honor my mother and father. I remember being frightened by what I might do. Could I ever again trust my own inclinations? Did I have an enemy buried secretly inside? I had been warned. I had to monitor and curtail my natural propensity for the common good. No champion of happiness arose to suggest that love and respect come directly from my nature. Although well-intended, the message asked me to seek guidance for my behavior outside and be suspicious of inclinations from within.

Later, as an adult, I learned a rather different, fanciful version of those commandments. An elderly scholar, who studied ancient texts, claimed the meanings of words had changed throughout the centuries, resulting in a distortion of our understanding of portions of those sacred writings.

Among the sections he reinterpreted in accordance with what he believed was their original meaning was the entire account of Moses receiving the tablets from God.

In effect, according to this scholar's interpretation, God's message from the heavens detailed how people would behave if they took him into their hearts. They would not kill. They would not steal. The commandments in this translation were not commandments at all but descriptions of how people would behave if they took God into their hearts. Men and women would then participate easily with each other in a most respectful and life-affirming manner. In no way does this version challenge the validity of current texts or translations, which might allow us to view the Ten Commandments as descriptive as well as prescriptive: "Thou shalt not [will not] kill." This unique perspective suggests a trust in people which might be wonderful for us to consider.

When we were students, codes of dress, peer pressure and teachers' guidance on how to think (and what to think) coerced us into becoming actors in our own lives, playing parts that we believed we should perform for our own self-preservation. We acquired and carried into adulthood masks which often didn't fit: the lover mask, the consumer mask, the business person mask, the bus driver mask, the secretary mask, the waiter/waitress mask. Each mask possessed its own rhythm or vibration. Sometimes, we could easily sense the dissonance between the mask's energy and our own inner rhythm. We withheld feelings, censored thoughts and denied intimacy in accordance with unwritten rules appropriate to each mask worn. Such denial breeds unhappiness, confusion and conflict. No wonder that young children, free of masks, when doing dialogues of self-exploration can always answer questions (they know how they feel, what they think and what they want), while adults often come to a dead end with the statement, "I don't know." We lose a sense of ourselves behind the masks.

In one family program we conducted, a teen-ager began to tackle his father playfully. The man backed away, declaring, "Hey, I'm your father, not one of your friends." A woman who came for a session talked about having wanted to be soft and gentle during a particular interview she conducted but she chose instead to uphold the professional detachment that she viewed as imperative in her job as personnel director. A credit officer in a bank spoke of how he had to ignore his instincts with people at his place of business; there, mathematical numbers and equations reigned supreme. A high school teacher talked about wanting to hug a student who had triumphed on a test after struggling all semester but restrained himself, reasoning that such personal gestures of affection had no place in the classroom.

What if we abandoned the roles? We wouldn't have to

abandon the activities we have chosen, but, once free of the masks, we could review and reconsider them from a happier place within. What if we listen more closely to our inner inclinations as we greet each situation? What if we drop the "shoulds," "have to's" and "musts" and replace them with innocence, spontaneity and curiosity?

We often uphold standards without questioning them. Most significantly, in the process we deny entire aspects of ourselves and squeeze the "bigness" of who we are into a tight, confining role. Ironically, we adjust to the confinement and then fear breaking through the barriers we helped erect.

I am not suggesting anarchy or the abandonment of responsibilities we have assumed. But could we be parents in the full bloom of who we are—open, honest, strong, vulnerable, sometimes clear and sometimes confused? As lovers, could we be authentic with our feelings, concerns and love, and be willing to tear down the walls of silence we may have built? As businessmen and women, could we value sincerity and "straight talk" as a powerful tool to build trust with clients, customers and coworkers? As students, could we share our intentions and concerns openly with our teachers (whomever they are) to help them and us enliven and make the educational process more pertinent and responsive? As medical patients, could we abandon all self-censorship and ask every doctor, every x-ray technician and every healthcare professional to deal with us and themselves in a respectful, open, honoring and, yes, loving manner? Even if we had no guarantee of results, how would it feel inside just to allow ourselves the full expression of who we are?

Years ago, a history professor of mine concluded after an in-depth study of armed conflict that most wars would have been avoided if each side knew exactly and completely how the other would respond to certain actions. In effect, lack of authenticity and full disclosure resulted usually in one group miscalculating the reaction of their opponent and blundering into offensive action and war. Authenticity could have global as well as personal advantages in fostering a harmonious and peaceful environment.

Those around us might not welcome our authenticity initially, but we could know that sharing ourselves without masks and filters can be a gift—for the other person and most certainly for ourselves. A wonderful example would be the actions of a seventeen-year-old boy named Sam, whom I wrote about in *A Land Beyond Tears.* Sam dared to break the silence and frozen smiles surrounding his mother's dying by asking her honest questions and, thereby, giving both of them as well as other members of his family opportunities to help each other, share deeply and find happiness even in what appeared to be a tragic situation.

A nurse I did sessions with feared that if she told her physician friends what she really thought about their procedures and bedside manners, they would disassociate themselves from her. As we continued exploring her concerns, the questions that arose became pinpointed. Did she want friends who valued her only when she censored herself and gave tacit approval for what she didn't believe in? Did she want to continue being dishonest and deny herself? When this woman acknowledged her discomfort with her masquerade, she decided her behavior had enriched neither herself nor her associates. Within days she discarded her mask and shared her observations and suggestions. To her surprise, many of the physicians appreciated her insights and asked for input on how they could make changes.

Someone in the audience at a seminar once asked me to comment on what I viewed as a key ingredient in my thirty-year love relationship with my wife. Rather innocently, I blurted an answer which drew wide-eyed stares. "Being with her is exactly like being alone," I said. When I realized the impact of my statement, I addressed the underlying meaning immediately. "What I wear, how my hair is combed, what I choose to do, whether I burp aloud or quietly, whether I am reclusive or extroverted, quiet or energetic are not issues when I am alone. I am and can be exactly who I am without judgments. When I am in the presence of this lady I share my life with, I feel the same delicious freedom that I feel when alone." Her love and acceptance of me and mine of her provide both of us with an open and nurturing environment which not only supports but champions personal authenticity.

Some claim that people pay a price for their authenticity. Indeed, at times, the immediate responses may not appear supportive. However, in this user-friendly universe, when our authenticity comes from happiness and love, the gain and lessons from such honest sharing and self-affirmation ultimately benefit both ourselves and those we address. In addition, we then tend to attract those who appreciate and want the same openness and authenticity.

When I first adopted the attitudinal perspective that we now teach and began to use gentle and nonjudgmental questions to dispel my personal baggage of discomforts, my thinking, values and responses to situations changed markedly. I ceased merely to negotiate with anxiety and anger in order to cope and adapt as I had previously done. Rather I began to re-order and, in fact, revolutionize my thinking/feeling apparatus. I scrutinized all the beliefs and judgments I had been taught as well as all those I had formulated for myself. So many appeared erroneous and self-defeating. I decided to hold on to only those which served me and those around me and to discard all the rest. In spite of psychotherapists and educators who claim we are victimized by the dictates of our unconscious and subconscious mind, I found I could probe every aspect of myself and change what I wanted in a wondrous act of re-creation. I could give birth to myself in accordance with the happiness and love I had come to value above all else. I had gently laid my past to rest. No longer a victim of my personal history (that's just a belief anyway), I had become a co-creator (with God) of an ever-evolving me.

While I celebrated this evolution, a very dear friend of mine made it clear that he found my personal changes appalling. Our relationship had spanned ten years. We had studied philosophy together as undergraduates at the same university. We carried the banners of civil rights through the streets of major cities. Together we had held hands with thousands of others protesting war. We shared a desire to see famine erased from the face of the earth, and we both supported self-help programs in developing nations. Several times each week, we discussed religion, philosophy, psychology, politics and science in long telephone conversations, and we socialized along with our wives just about every weekend. Throughout those years, anger, anguish, self-righteous indignation and sadness accompanied those outpourings of energy and concern for our planet. We never questioned these emotions, since we assumed they reflected the sincerity and depth of our commitments. However, as I became happier and more accepting of myself and those around me, my discomfort and emotional fury subsided, though my concern and participation continued. I could now hold up a poster of protest without screaming. I could help different racial groups in their search for equality without damning those who were prejudiced. I wanted to understand rather than condemn. I wanted to build bridges between friends rather than walls between enemies.

My friend found my revised position alarming. At first he

accused me of not caring. But then, as he watched me continue to lend my support, he dropped this charge and accused me instead of having become emotionally numb, since I no longer greeted current instances of injustice with what he considered appropriate unhappiness. Human intelligence, he argued, demanded such a reaction.

In response to this assertion, I raised some questions. "If we are working for peace, wouldn't it be important for us to feel peaceful inside?" "If we condemn those who are prejudiced, aren't we then ourselves demonstrating yet another act of prejudice?" "Why do we believe we have to be angry in order to precipitate change?" He attacked my inquiry as inappropriate. He objected to my altered attitude and hated my questions. Even if I only asked them aloud to myself in order to increase my own clarity and understanding, he would shake his head with obvious annoyance.

One Sunday morning, my friend and his wife joined my family for breakfast in our home. He had just read an article about the growing backlash to the civil rights movement. As he shared information from his reading, he raged against what he called the stupidity of some legislators. At one point, he even banged on the table with his fist. I guess he believed he had "right" on his side.

"Why are you getting yourself so angry?" I asked softly.

"Because I want to! Is that all right with you?" he barked.

"Sure," I replied, touching his arm. "It's fine. But I still wonder why you want to feel that way here and now."

He pushed my hand away. "Listen, if you ask me one more damn question, I'm leaving! And I won't ever come back."

I searched myself before responding. I had loved this man and valued our friendship for years. At the same time, my questions had become my tool for learning. Just as I accepted him with his anger and fury, I wanted him to be open to the evolving, inquiring me. In effect, he demanded that I stop being me. Bottom line: He wanted me to be the person he thought I should be rather than the one I had become. I now asked myself, did I want to spend hours, weeks, even years censoring myself in order to placate his anger? And, truly, was my friendship of use to him if I presented a limited or dishonest picture of myself? I wanted the ease of authenticity for both of us in our relationship; thus, I chose to ask another question.

"Why would you leave here and never come back if I asked you one more question?"

He never replied. He grabbed his wife's hand, rose from the chair and left our home abruptly.

That event occurred fifteen years ago. My friend kept his word; he never saw or spoke to me again. I knew in the very moment that I posed the question that I had made a choice to value authenticity (the freedom to be me) over self-suppression. I realized that I would rather be alone than wear a mask that no longer fit. I never mourned the passing of that relationship. I only hoped that the experience of those years of communion had been as meaningful and useful to him as they had been to me.

The curtain had been raised. Although I had no intention of being the grand inquisitor to all those I met, I did want to express myself more freely and completely with those who chose to be with me. Sure, some people walked away. I guess to those wanting their unhappiness and anger reinforced, I no longer appeared attractive. My intention had set me on a different path.

However, other people gathered around. We discovered each other and created exciting new friendships based on acceptance, respect and love. We cherished each other as we were rather than as we wanted the other person to be. The letting go of that one key relationship in my life marked a coming of age in which I began putting my trust more fully in my journey to happiness.

The risk we associate with authenticity is illusory. The more we nurture ourselves, remove the masks and allow ourselves uncensored expression, the more the rhythms within blend with those surrounding us. We create inner-outer harmony. Personal authenticity leads us to abandon the masks and masquerades we do not truly own so that we can embrace and celebrate our most central character. We give up only the laborious task of playing the games. In effect, we simplify our lives. One face greets every situation without embarrassment or regret. Rather than rehearse the "right" response, we can trust ourselves by allowing the response we feel in any given moment. Some people interpret such a perspective as a "license to kill"—to be rude and attacking. What materializes suggests quite the opposite. Unhappy commentaries are not signs of authenticity; they are signs of unhappiness. My experience teaches me that increased openness and honesty enhance a sense of personal ease and inner harmony. With that growing river of comfort (happiness) comes increased respect and love for those around us.

This doorway to happiness opens easily. We can begin by sharing with a lover, a friend, a coworker, a son or daughter or parent some fact about ourselves we might have kept secret or, at least, shared rarely with others. The very next time we edit ourselves in a conversation, we can override that impulse and allow our thoughts and feelings to be expressed. And, as we begin now to share more freely our concerns, we may also begin now to smile more freely at a child or hold out our hand more easily to a stranger. These acts, too, can be wondrous expressions of personal authenticity.

Shortcut # 3—Letting Go of Judgments

Of all the shortcuts to happiness, letting go of judgments can be the most dazzling. By discarding judgments and embracing people and situations more openly, we not only provide ourselves with opportunities for great happiness but also sometimes pierce walls formerly viewed as impenetrable.

During one of our Son-Rise Program[SM] meetings with the parents of a special child exhibiting severe difficulties with gross motor coordination, we pooled information and observations in order to establish teaching baselines for the home-based, child-centered program this family would soon establish. We expressed our desire to take cues from this little person, using her preferences and inclinations to guide us in helping her.

In the course of our sharing, one staff member, Bonnie, talked enthusiastically about Katie's participation in their sessions together and the strides she had made. "She's a little unsure of herself when she walks. Yet she took three firm steps in my direction during our morning session," she reported.

Annie, another staff member, raised her hand, bubbling with her usual excitement. "Katie went even further this afternoon. While she and I played with hand puppets, she giggled and reached for the one on my right arm. I invited her to come and get it if she wanted. She took almost five full steps to reach me. She's a real plugger!"

Katie's father leaned forward, aghast, and said, "But my daughter doesn't walk."

"Oh," Annie said respectfully, "I didn't know that."

Judgments about people and possibilities limit our thinking and what we might try to accomplish. With the very best of intentions, we try to use judgments as powerful tools to help safeguard ourselves and those we love. We want to be able to distinguish between "good" and "bad," "right" and "wrong," "possible" and "impossible" in order to help us make decisions and choose behaviors. And yet, our rush to judgment usually distances us from the possibility of changing and creating personal miracles in our lives and cements us into being "stuck" in our unhappiness.

We learned to judge as children. Just as we absorbed beliefs without question from our parents and friends, from politicians, religious leaders and the media, so also we learned unquestioningly to judge just about everyone and everything in our world. We spend most of our lives judging—our love relationships, our finances, our sexuality, our parenting and our self-worth. Then we turn the lens of our scrutinizing eye toward other people and toward events.

We are a gifted organism capable of responding to a vast

and complex series of stimuli, be it a lover's comment, lower back pain, a child's report card, a bounced check, stale bread, rush-hour traffic, stock-market fluctuations, air pollution, news of anti-abortion or pro-choice demonstrations, drug trafficking or political unrest in other countries. We filter these stimuli through our beliefs and make judgments about what we see, hear and experience.

The following might appear at first to be an oversimplistic view of human behavior; however, as a way to gather further insight, we might be able to reduce all human concerns to one essential question that we tend to ask ourselves repetitiously. "Is this good for me or is this bad for me?" Our answer to that question triggers a variety of feelings and actions.

For example, someone might declare his or her love for us. Immediately, we engage some version of the question—is this person's declaration of caring and intimacy good or bad for me? One possible answer might be yes, this is good (the judgment), now I can feel valued (the feeling) and we can get married (the action). Or, an alternative conclusion could be: this is bad for me (the judgment) because I will now feel pressured (the feeling) to commit more time and energy to this relationship so I better leave to preserve my freedom (the action).

Very simply, the stimulus (in this case the declaration of love) does not create happiness or unhappiness; the stimulus just is! How we *judge* it determines how we feel and how we act. If we judge a circumstance to be good (for us, for those we love, for humanity), we feel excited, happy, fulfilled and tend to support or move toward the experience. If we judge it as bad, then we feel duly angry, fearful, anxious or sad and tend to move away from the experience.

Frequently, our judgments surface so quickly that we are not fully aware of ever posing the question (Is it good or bad for me?). Nevertheless, the question, in spirit if not in fact, always underlies our judgment and guides much of the emotional experiences and choices we make.

Not only do we tend to render easy opinions on just about every subject, we have learned to judge from a particular bias: We have become geniuses in pinpointing all that's difficult and bad in our lives and the world around us. The media reflect and reinforce that bias. The reward for such studious vigilance results in continual stress, discomfort and anxiety. We set ourselves up for unhappiness rather than for peace or comfort.

One morning, I did sessions with a married couple in which the wife voiced her unhappiness because her husband did not push for more sexual contact. In the afternoon of that very same day, another woman expressed displeasure in the face of her husband's push for "too much" sexual contact. In our workshops, I am dazzled always to hear members of the group talk about feeling cheated and deprived because they don't have enough money while people sitting right beside them express feelings of guilt or discomfort because they have too much money. If the stock market drops, we get unhappy and mourn our losses. If the stock market goes up, we worry about when to sell and how to hold on to our gains. We demonstrate an uncanny ability to turn any set of circumstances into an opportunity to be uncomfortable or unhappy. No sinister motives fuel such a decision-making process. Unwittingly, we have been misled by a culture that has taught us systematically to use discomfort at almost every juncture as the best way to take care of ourselves.

As a result, our delights can be few and fleeting. We might celebrate success when we reach a goal, but then we turn promptly and cautiously to the next unfolding "problem." Frequently, we view ourselves as responders to or victims of situations rather than as authors of our experiences. As a result, we can easily lose our way and become confused with our entire thinking process, condemning it erroneously for robbing us of inner peace and tranquility.

Following from such conclusions, massive numbers of teachers, therapists and seminar facilitators in personal growth and spiritual development suggest "not thinking" as the pathway to enlightenment and/or heaven. They throw out the baby with the bathwater.

In contrast, we could be grateful for all our skills and talents and use them for our benefit. We could, in fact, harness our capability to create beliefs and make judgments as a tool to grease the wheels of our own personal liberation from discomfort.

———

The contemporary mythology of happiness suggests that pleasurable feelings germinate from the "heart" or intuitive side of our brain. People insist that we can't think our way to happiness, that joy and delight bubble forth from our instinctive, soul-like nature. Hmmmm.

In the last two decades, studies conducted by neurosurgeons and neuroscientists regarding the language capability of stroke victims and other neurologically-impaired people have led to amazing revelations about the brain. First studies showed the left hemisphere (left side of the cerebral cortex) appeared to be the seat of abstract learning, symbolic language, logical thinking, sequential reasoning, beliefs and judgments and the right hemisphere to contain more intuitive, instinctive, pictorial and spatial operations. In effect, left brain function seemed to foster analytical thinking while right brain function appeared to nurture our artistic, musical, spiritual and visionary capabilities. Further research into these distinct segments of brain geography suggested that happiness must originate in the "beingness" of who we are, which scientists believed to be governed by right-brain function. Although new evidence now indicates an overlapping of activities in both these areas of the brain, clinicians still view the general demarcation of the brain into two parts as valid.

Many current philosophies and psychologies have

made our analytical left brain capability the enemy and claim that ignoring or silencing that aspect of our thinking process would lead to clarity or true happiness. New slogans have arisen in the culture. "You're too much in your head (left brain)." "Stop thinking (left brain) and start feeling (right brain)." "You think too much (left brain)." "Get real (right brain)." Yet society continues fervently to reward the logical, analytical thinking of doctors, lawyers, bankers, architects, business leaders and teachers. However, many of us personally have grown suspicious of the coolness of thought (logical, linear thinking), striving to realize more fully the romantic, intuitive and "feeling" aspects of our nature.

In doing so, we have bypassed a key dynamic in dispensing with unhappiness. Misery as a human experience comes from judging ourselves, other people and events as bad or terrible for us. *We can say quite accurately that we have "thought" ourselves into unhappiness with our judgments, and we can think ourselves back out by examining them and letting them go.* How could we hope to be happy while distrusting a significant portion of our mental apparatus? Acceptance and utilization, not condemnation, of the miracle of consciousness and our ability to reason will lead us to happiness.

An instrument of recent medical invention, Positron Emission Tomography (P.E.T.), utilized by behavioral researchers has opened new doorways to our understanding of the brain and its functioning. Via P.E.T. scanning, researchers have created computer-generated color graphics of the brain in action. Glucose molecules, joined with radioactive isotopes, are injected intravenously into the bloodstream. The brain metabolizes the glucose through its activity, thereby releasing gamma rays from the isotopes which the P.E.T. scanner reads. The intensity of color generated reveals to scientists what part of the brain is most active during different operations.

In one experiment, researchers flashed a series of photographs before participants in their study. One series contained heartwarming, inspiring photos of families, lovers, mothers with children and beautiful landscapes. When watching events that stimulated happiness and comfort, their left brain became extraordinarily active. When participants watched scenes which they reported generated fear, anxiety and discomfort in them, their so-called visionary right brain cells become noticeably engaged. Thus, the seat of happiness to everyone's surprise appeared to be the left brain rather than the right and our capacity for happiness to be very much entwined with our ability to think and make judgments (or let go of them). Upon seeing photographs which pleased them, the participants apparently engaged or actively disengaged some component of the logical, linear thought process which produced peace, comfort and happiness.

Suddenly, a new question surfaces. If the keys to happiness (the ability to allow, generate and sustain it) lie within our left brain thinking and are related to the way we think and adopt beliefs, how can we learn to use these left brain functions to serve us more effectively?

Easy! A quick decision to challenge and change the judgments we make will yield awesome results. Rather than deny or dismiss what we do best (form judgments and make beliefs), why not harness our mental apparatus to serve us by dismantling judgments and/or beliefs which lead to unhappiness and conflict? I cannot envision any action more deeply exciting and romantic than taking conscious charge of this uniquely human and creative ability. *The secret to happiness lies not in events but in our responses to them.*

During my first year of college, I shared a room with a student from Asia. As I exited a class one day, an administrator met me and informed me that my roommate's eleven-year-old sister had just died in an automobile accident. I remember being startled by the intrusion into my world of one of life's inevitabilities. At the same time, I could hardly comprehend a child's dying.

I catapulted down several flights of stairs and ran across the campus in order to reach my friend and offer my assistance, aware, at the same time, of my stomach juices gushing up into my throat. Death! When my grandfather had died years before, various members of my family collapsed in anguish and sorrow. My grandmother, hysterical with grief, actually jumped into the grave after the coffin was lowered. Images ripped through my mind like jagged edges of broken glass. When I arrived at the dormitory, I realized I did not know what to say or how to act. I imagined consoling my friend, but I wasn't quite sure how to do it. Was I to hug him, cry with him or curse the universe with him? My God, I thought, he had to face the death of his younger sister, just a child, while he himself had only marked his nineteenth birthday.

The doorway to our room loomed before me like the entrance to some inescapable catastrophe. Pausing with my hand on the knob, I drew three deep breaths and then entered. Dom sat quietly on his bed, his legs neatly folded under him. A small candle burned brightly in a dish on his desk. He smiled easily. No anguish or discomfort marred his expression. In that moment, I contemplated the worst of all possibilities: he didn't know about his sister yet. Could I tell him?

"Dom, um, . . ." I hesitated. "Dom, I have to tell you . . . well, I really don't know how to . . . er, do you know about? . . ." Inept would have been a kind word for my presentation.

His smile broadened in the face of my faltering speech. "Yes," he said calmly, "I know." Then, to my surprise, he talked about the wonder of his sister's passing. In accordance with his religious doctrine, he believed she had become one with God and the universe. In fact, he sensed her closer now than in life. I needn't be sad, he assured me. The candle, he explained, celebrated her transition into another dimension. Something had been gained, not lost, by the accident that took her life. To my utter amazement, he was genuinely happy. Everything about him indicated a profound sense of tranquility and peace of mind.

The experience revolutionized my understanding of human nature and the human condition. Previously, I had thought any caring person would be grief-stricken when faced with the death of someone he loved, as if that specific response had been genetically encoded in everyone. Dom showed me a different way. The obvious conclusion: Our reactions and experiences follow from our beliefs and judgments. Thus, death finalized in a cemetery in Brooklyn might be brooding and painful, while one honored on a hillside in Nepal might be joyful and easy. Our viewpoint determines our experience. Even though, when I was a college freshman, I might have viewed death as the most difficult of human events, others had the capability, I realized, of embracing it quite differently. Death is neither good nor bad until we judge it so. And we judge it in accordance with cultural, religious and personal biases. Why do we do this? To take care of ourselves and to be respectful of others in the best way we know how at the moment.

Our staff once worked with a family whose child had

difficulty speaking and controlling his limbs as a result of cerebral palsy. The parents judged their son's differences as terrible. They mourned for the child he might have been rather than embracing the child he was. As they let go of their judgments that his condition was bad, they began to discover the beauty and genius of their little boy in his heroic efforts to interact and communicate with others. They discovered God in an illness they had believed previously to have its source in sin and evil.

A forty-five-year-old woman who had attended one of our workshops and then continued exploring in individual sessions protested her cancer diagnosis and subsequent treatment. "Why me?" she cried. Her adult life had been one of quiet desperation, and now she had to endure battling this life-threatening illness. Although she declared herself a victim of her husband's insensitivity and her children's disrespect, she could not believe that the universe would similarly victimize her. During her explorations, she began to realize how she had been consistently silent and passive when others expressed their wishes to her. Even her part-time employment represented settling for work she disliked. As she untangled the web of judgments of her cancer, herself and her family, a new clarity and self-respect unfolded. She stopped judging her cancer, became dramatically more assertive in codetermining treatment procedures with her doctors, and initiated healthy changes in her relationships with family members. In doing so, she turned a crisis into a challenge and an opportunity. She changed her vision and, in the process, changed her life.

During our last session together, she turned to me cheerfully and said, "Bears, I can't believe I am going to say this, but my cancer has been the best thing that ever happened to me." She giggled at her own statement, then continued, "Next time the universe gives me such a gift, I'm not going to be depressed and spend months protesting. I'll just change my attitude and decide to be happy with . . . whatever! But next time I won't wait; I'll do it at the onset. I'll open my arms instead of putting on boxing gloves." She had taken what others might deem misfortune and used it for her benefit and growth. Most significantly, this woman's simple decision not to judge her cancer would give a new, happier shape to all her future life experiences.

Two professional career and placement counselors loved the ideas expressed in our books and our work. As a result, they seized on the notion of questioning judgments and letting them go as a personal inspiration and a useful strategy to help their clients reframe the realities of unemployment and the search for new jobs or careers. They helped people take the seemingly difficult experience of being fired, laid off or forced into early retirement and turn it into an opportunity of a lifetime. Too young? Too old? Too much experience? Too little experience? One by one, they helped their clients convert what others judged as liabilities into dynamic assets they could market successfully. An older executive can add a seasoned perspective to the hustle-bustle of the moment and help companies make more effective, long-range plans. Younger managers can bring with them vitality and an evolving business style that could easily be molded to fit within the corporate culture.

A negative assumption only meant a person had not yet discovered the wonder and possibility for success in their new situation. With supportive enthusiasm and professional savvy in their work and in a book they co-authored, these two career counselors encouraged others to challenge the short-circuits that judged circumstances as bad and to take concrete steps that demonstrated their value to prospective employers, helping them to secure lucrative new jobs.

We are the belief makers! We can find the best or create the best in each and every situation. The "good" and the "bad" and what follows (the happiness or the misery) are products of our judgments—pure and simple!

What do we do in the face of this reality? We can take hours, weeks, months or even years to work through our complex network of beliefs and certainly find the journey to be wonderful and worthwhile. We could also simply change the dynamics of our beliefs now by basing our decisions and actions on our wanting to be happy. We can take the same skill at making judgments and use it to our advantage. Instead of viewing events as bad for us, we can decide now to see them as good for us or, at the very least, useful opportunities to learn and benefit from.

A woman who had made such a decision as a result of these ideas told me later how she greeted a surprise that life soon brought her—a fire that destroyed her home and all her possessions. At one o'clock in the morning, she stood barefoot in the street with her husband, her son and her daughter, shivering from the cold night air as she watched firemen hopelessly battle a blaze which rapidly consumed their house. An art collection acquired over twenty years of traveling became dust. The flames destroyed treasured gifts, favorite pieces of furniture and photographs, as well as videos documenting all the years of their family life. The mementos of her past disappeared right before her eyes.

In those first moments, she tensed, overcome by the event. Then she remembered her decision to drop judgments. "Okay," she told herself, "now is the time!" She pulled her husband and children closer and whispered, "We're alive. We're all alive. Isn't that just wonderful?" Her daughter smiled. Her son nodded, then sighed his relief. The tension in her husband's face dissipated. Then this woman eyed what remained of her home and said a silent good-bye to all the souvenirs of her personal history.

When the walls of her house collapsed, she smiled like a little girl watching fireworks. She had let go of all judgments.

She would face the next day, she decided, by welcoming the new circumstances which this event precipitated. Her ease inspired both family and friends to view the situation hopefully. From the ashes came the clear awareness that she possessed always the freedom to be happy. When she dropped that first, fleeting judgment of "bad," she swam easily in the river of life, liberated by her new lesson and the life-affirming vision she had invoked.

Deciding to embrace an experience without judgments leaves us open to finding elements in every event that serve and teach us. If judging people and experiences as bad brings unhappiness (fear, anxiety, anguish, impatience, anger, sadness), why not put our judgments to work for us by flipping the perspective? We don't necessarily have to abandon judging entirely (although doing so might create the most optimal, childlike perspective of curiosity and enjoyment); we could at least change our bias.

We could begin by judging everything as good and then grow into letting go of judgments completely. The stock market crashes and I lose my equity. How wonderful! What an opportunity not to rely on my investments! My wife announces she wants to leave me. Perfect! I can trust this will be best for her, the children and me. My employer fires me without notice. How interesting! This can be my chance to re-evaluate who I am and what I really want. My child blames me for making her unhappy. Wow! What a fascinating idea! Her statement challenges me to question who is responsible for our personal happiness; my search for an answer can only enrich me.

What I am posing might appear comical at first. The impact, however, will be quite amazing and immediate. Our revised personal and global vision will produce supporting evidence. Look for what is good and we will discover it. Just pointing ourselves in such a direction will give us new eyes and new ears. If we let go of judgments of people and events as bad, we usher in a time of miracles and wonder. We will find what we seek!

As I conclude this section, I would like to address what might appear as an inconsistency. Suggesting we see something as good could sound just as judgmental as damning people or events as bad. Certainly, we can note two sides to the coin of judgment. Does letting go of judgments mean making the assessment something is good? No! However, I have used this frame of reference in response to observing what happier people do easily and whimsically to support their happiness.

Letting go of judgments means adopting an accepting attitude. People have always challenged my wife and me as well as others we have trained about the paradox of acceptance. If we accept a person or situation as it is, they argue, we will become passive, lethargic and the world will not change. From that viewpoint, being accepting and nonjudgmental appears quite unattractive. However, the same critics also note the energy and enthusiasm people display in altering their circumstances. How do we explain such a paradox? Truly accepting a person or a set of circumstances feels like letting go in the most gentle and liberating way, a joyful movement inward that frees us from unhappiness. Unencumbered by the judgments which cause anxiety, anger and fear, we find a reservoir of energy more expansive than ever imagined.

Acceptance frees us to use all our resources, including those previously consumed by unhappiness, in a direct and powerful thrust. My wife and I had such an experience during those rigorous and wonderful years in which we worked with our once autistic son seven days a week, twelve hours each day. Acceptance allowed us to see more, love more and have more energy to make a difference.

Upon reflection, we did what we hear others say they do over and over again when they are happy. We let go of judgments that our child's autistic condition was terrible and accepted him completely, without reservations. Soon after, we began to see the situation as a golden opportunity to help a lost little boy.

We do not have to judge in order to set direction and

priorities. We do not have to label people, places or events in order to decide how to respond. We can just follow our wants!

Once we have made the choice personally, as best we can, to greet situations with a nonjudgmental, accepting attitude, we can then, with our adopted bias, embrace whatever the universe delivers as good. Such a position does not reflect a moral standard or any verifiable truth. We use it simply as a reminder of the possibilities and happiness any of us can create in response to any circumstance.

Whether we learned (or deduced) our biases thirty years ago, three days ago or three minutes ago has no bearing on our ability to change them now in whatever way we choose. We empower our judgments at the moment we make them. We can retrain ourselves by decision. We can dump the old judgments like dusty plates from old cupboard shelves and refuse to make new ones. We can begin anew today, right now. Just decide. Choose a nonjudgmental stance in the next moment or decide to see the next event and those thereafter as opportunities for something meaningful and wonderful even in the face of contrary evidence. That's all it takes!

Let go of the judgments and we will fly on the wings of acceptance, love and happiness!

Shortcut # 4—Being Present

Unhappiness does not exist in the present moment! Though at first glance this statement might appear preposterous, the underlying insight creates yet another shortcut. Unhappiness exists only as a reflection or regret about the past or as an anticipation or worry toward the future. It does not exist right now, in this moment . . . if we stay in this moment.

At first, this concept might appear paradoxical. Whatever we choose as the subject of our attention at any given time will occur in "this moment." Thus we could conclude that we are always in the moment, always present! For example, as we drive a vehicle along a highway at fifty-five miles per hour, we might daydream about a relationship or new business venture. Certainly, we can see ourselves as "in the moment" with our daydream; however, we are clearly not "in the moment" or present with our driving. An awesome number of traffic accidents and fatalities result from our not being present as we drive our vehicles.

While dining in a restaurant with friends, we might allow our focus of attention to drift from the conversation to thoughts of the next day's chores. We can be said to be "in the moment" with our contemplation, but not "in the moment" or present with our friends and their conversation. The resulting inattention to our friends creates distance between ourselves and them. Long-term internal meanderings can subvert trust and intimacy between people (one member of a relationship or business association "checks out" during significant exchanges). In addition to eroding the quality of interactions, we miss relevant information as well as various pleasures our experiences offer us. When we eat a meal inattentively, for example, our teeth grind the food and we swallow, but we hardly taste what we eat and barely notice the quantity we shovel into our mouths. Obesity can be one side effect of not being present with the chosen activity of consuming food. How many of us eat while conversing, reading or watching television or when we are "on the run" from one involvement to another? Unconscious consumption not only sabotages the pleasure of eating, but also can result in mindless excess.

Even before we approach "being present" as a powerful shortcut to happiness, we can readily begin to see the impact of *not* being present. A pilot drinks alcoholic beverages prior to take-off and then jokes easily with his copilot and navigator in the cockpit of a commercial jetliner instead of being fully present with his instruments. The result: a major air disaster. A surgeon takes a series of phone calls while flipping through a patient's records rather than being present with every detail in the file. The result: he administers drugs to which the person has known life-threatening allergies. An electrician rushes to complete her job instead of being present as she checks each and every wired connection. The result: an electrical fire. A carpenter watches nearby women and passing cars instead of being present as he nails a column to a porch. The result: a pulverized finger and a less-than-secure platform support. A parent half listens to his child's communication instead of being present to a request for help or guidance. The result: the youngster feels abandoned even in the presence of her parents and seeks answers elsewhere, which may prove more muddled than those her parents could have suggested. A lover worries about his or her upcoming sexual performance rather than being present with his or her partner. The result: an aloofness from the experience which reduces pleasure and might lead to frigidity or impotence.

We compromise a substantial portion of our daily experience by choosing not to be present with our current activities.

A staff member in her early thirties made her participation at our teaching center progressively more difficult for herself with each passing year. Julie wanted a meaningful and lasting relationship, which she had not yet developed. She began worrying about the possible fading of her attractiveness as well as the decreasing number of years left for childbearing. After all, she reminded herself, if she had already lived thirty-three years without having married, the possibility existed that she might live thirty-three more years the same way. The embarrassment of such an eventuality seemed unthinkable to her. Not only did she have visions during the day of being alone, despite the fact she lived in a teaching community of thirty people, many of whom loved her dearly, but she had elaborate dreams at night of ending her days as a disease-infested bag lady on the anonymous streets of some unknown city.

Julie's desire for a relationship became an obsession. Her lack of personal fulfillment began to affect all her daily activities. Although she had proved to be a gifted teacher and mentor for adults as well as children, she became unhappy in her work. Her living situation no longer appeared ideal to her. She decided nothing in her life had real value without a special relationship. Every moment became a chance to peer into a bleak future. Day and night, throughout every activity, she maintained a mystical vigil for the certain "someone" she wanted to appear. No wonder she did not find her life fulfilling; she no longer stayed present with the work she had once loved so ardently.

One day while I was reviewing a program design with Julie, an idea occurred to me.

"What would happen," I asked her, "if you knew that, in six months, Prince Charming, the perfect person you have been seeking, would appear? You would recognize him; he would recognize you, and a relationship would develop." Julie eyed me carefully, scrutinizing my face and my words. I continued, "How would you feel if I told you that within six months this person would be here?"

Julie leaned back in her chair and grinned. "Well, that would be great!" she said. "Really great!"

"Okay," I added. "What if I told you it would take a year? One year from now that person would be here for you?"

She smiled and shook her head affirmatively. "That would be great too. If I knew that in one year I would begin a meaningful relationship, that would be fine."

I decided to see if I could extend the time frame a bit further. "What if it took two years? You would wait two more years, but then that special person would appear in your life."

Julie sighed, smiled again and responded, "Okay, two years would be fine, too. If I could count on having the relationship I want in two years, then that would be fine. Actually, I could be patient in that case. So, sure it would be fine . . . it would be great."

I pulled a piece of stationery from my desk drawer and said aloud what I began to write. "I guarantee personally that within two years you will have the relationship you want." Then I signed my name and pushed the paper in front of her.

Julie looked down at my note, lowered her glasses and stared at me. "Oh, c'mon, Bears!" she blurted.

"Wait," I replied directly. "I am guaranteeing personally that you will have the relationship you want within the next two-year period."

She cocked her head. "Are you serious?"

"Absolutely. Very serious."

"I don't believe you," she said playfully.

As I reached to withdraw the paper, she grabbed it. "Well, I'll take it just in case." Then she left.

During the next few days, a rather marvelous transformation occurred in Julie. At first, I dismissed my own initial observations, believing myself to be biased. However, others also began noticing changes in her. Julie's level of enthusiasm with children rose noticeably. She displayed a new insightfulness in our programs for adults, making herself a more significant staff contributor. Even clients and workshop participants found her attentiveness and concern compelling. With each passing week, her level of happiness grew. In addition, I could not help but notice how focused she had become, conscious about every detail in all the individual and group workshops. Her changes stunned the entire teaching staff.

About one month after presenting her with my guarantee, I sat down with Julie once again. "How are you doing?" I asked.

"Oh, great!" she answered. "Just great!"

"I'm really excited for you. But Julie, could you explain exactly what's great?"

"Sure. Working with the kids has been so fulfilling and inspiring. Andy. Jessica. Tony. Lisa. Laura. I have enjoyed each moment with them. I also feel my work with groups has improved. Each time I guide a class, I feel more on top of the action. Nothing gets by me now. I feel more useful to the participants and I really love that."

"Wow," I exclaimed. "You are amazing! How come all this has happened for you?"

She laughed self-consciously. "Well, for one thing, I don't think about my relationship in the future anymore. When I am really here with what I am doing, it's fun and very, very, satisfying. I've even been enjoying my apartment more." She giggled.

"That's wonderful!" I responded. "Do you still have that piece of paper that I gave you with my guarantee?"

She chuckled. "Sure, I carry it with me." She pulled it out of her pocketbook and gave it to me.

I took it in my hand. "Okay. You have learned what there was to learn from a guarantee, so now I am going to cancel it. Okay?"

She hesitated for a moment, then nodded her head and said, "Fine."

I crumpled the note and tossed it into the wastepaper basket.

When I saw Julie the next day, she appeared miserable. Apparently, she had shifted her focus from being present with each current endeavor to worrying about the future once again. However, after a lapse of almost a week she changed again. A note from her affirmed her learning. "No more guarantees. I realized how to take care of my future today . . . be present and be happy now. I heard you say it many times, but this time I am saying it. Thanks for playing with me. Love, Julie."

A framed poster of a seated old man, leaning forward with his chin on his hand, hangs in the office of a friend. The quote offered below this burdened form reads, "I have worried about many things in my life . . . most of which never happened."

On many occasions, I work with people who deal continuously with pain (physical as well as emotional). Most of us find the sensation of pain to be very present and compelling. Although we may have read first-person accounts of people in accidents or combat who endured grave injuries but felt no pain until they reached points of safety, those special experiences do not seem applicable to the circumstances of our daily lives. However, I had a very intriguing experience with a man in physical distress who came to do sessions concerning his marital problems.

During the first few minutes of our meeting, he stated that he suffered from severe, chronic lower back pain. Although he tried not to use much medication, he said he would if the need arose during our walk. Twenty minutes later, Doug announced he had to stop the session to take a pill. He had begun to experience severe pain, which radiated from his back down into his left leg. Frantically, he removed a miniature flask filled with water from one pocket and a vial of capsules from another. I stood quietly beside him, asking if I could help in any way. He shook his head. Finally, he brought two pills in one hand and the water container in the other toward his mouth. His face, which had become contorted by pain, began to relax even before he inserted anything into his mouth. As he gulped down the pills, his entire demeanor changed immediately.

"How do you feel?" I asked.

"Oh, much better," Doug sighed.

I watched with naive astonishment. "How did the pill have such an impact even before you put it in your mouth?"

He laughed. "Does seem strange, doesn't it?" He continued our walk as if pain free.

"How do you account for such speedy action?" I probed.

"Well, my doctor told me it would take the medication about twenty to thirty minutes to ease the pain."

"Then how do you explain the immediate relief?"

"I guess," he said, "because I know the pain will go away in twenty minutes, it doesn't feel so bad anymore."

"Do you still have the pain right now?" I inquired.

"Oh, yes," he said matter-of-factly. "But it's going to go away very soon. I'm not unhappy about it anymore. Actually, Bears, as I say that I realize it doesn't really hurt as much as before."

As Doug explored further, he discovered part of the discomfort or unhappiness with his lower back pain came from his belief that it would continue indefinitely. Each time it began, he would resurrect the same fear of future pain, until, of course, he took his medication. In his unfolding moment-to-moment experience, his pain was not a cause of unhappiness; only when he made projections into the future, did he fill himself with discomfort. Later he concluded, if he wanted to be happy, he had merely to decide to be here now, in the present moment.

The senior officer of a major manufacturing company, who attended one of our programs, realized that as a result of his chronic thrust to do two or more activities at once he never brought himself completely into the present moment. He spoke as if he split his consciousness into sections. When people talked, he read his mail. He used hand motions to give instructions to secretaries and assistants while engaged in phone conversations with employees. A furious note taker, he jotted down endless ideas for the sales and marketing departments while trying to listen to reports delivered by key personnel on other matters.

Although he defended his actions by noting his successes, he did admit, finally, to feeling stressed and dissatisfied with his daily work experience. In fact, he realized that as Chief Operating Officer, he had inspired his managing executives to act similarly. Nobody really listened to each other. Oh yes, everyone mimicked the pose of attention. People had their eyes open; they faced the speaker at strategy meetings and sales conferences, but they appeared anything but captivated and were quite routinized in their responses.

Thomas vowed, on his return home, to incorporate immediately some of the central lessons he had learned at The Option Institute. Among all the varied components of "a vision to live by" that we discussed, he loved the idea of being present as his major personal and, perhaps, corporate tool to gain greater satisfaction and happiness.

Several vice-presidents noted with surprise that he no longer read his mail or leafed through the morning financial statements as he spoke with them. At the opening of a strategy meeting, he decided to lead a guided meditation (as we had done together at the Institute) with his managers so they could relax and focus their attention on the material at hand. There were quizzical smiles around the conference table; however, everyone cooperated. At the end of the meeting, several of his key employees thanked him for the three-minute meditation, acknowledging how they had benefited by those few minutes of quiet, peaceful internal reflection. As a result, they reported feeling more present and alert.

Excited by the possibilities of such a simple idea, Thomas introduced the notion of being present to his line managers. They created a campaign to inspire all employees to commit themselves to being more "in the moment." Thomas noted three distinct benefits which he could measure. First, people acted genuinely more interested and excited in what they did. Second, efficiency increased. And third, job-related accidents decreased.

His sales personnel used the concept as a tool to reconceive some of their interpersonal marketing techniques, also with noticeable results. Being present allowed them not only to listen attentively, but also to respond in more respectful, useful and innovative ways. The company became more responsive to modifying products to their customer's requirements and orders increased. One customer asked Thomas whether he had sent his salespeople to charm school.

Over the years, he sent administrators, production coordinators and customer service representatives to our seminars in an effort to strengthen his program and incorporate authenticity, gratitude, letting go of judgments and other aspects of "a vision to live by" into his corporate culture. In addition, he loved using nonjudgmental questions as a tool to intensify communication among department managers and open new doorways in research and development.

What started for Thomas as a decision to improve the quality of his own personal life became a basis of a business ethic which, additionally, improved the effectiveness, vitality and profit of his company as well as the level of satisfaction of his employees. Becoming happier, a pursuit worthy in itself, had become a powerful force in the marketplace.

Thomas called his newly adopted vision a "win-win" decision for both those in his company and those they served.

I worked once, over a period of time, with a woman whose parents had been survivors of the Holocaust during World War II. Their traumatic experiences had affected the rest of their lives. The phantoms of dead family members and friends haunted their every waking hour. Their experiences of killings, torture and starvation in the concentration camps left them with scars they said would never heal. In fact, they insisted they wanted to keep their memories alive to ensure that such an inhuman atrocity never be repeated. Their daughter had taken up their torch, adopting their phantoms and making their memories part of her own past. As a result, she admitted, she had difficulties enjoying her marriage and her children. First, though she lived in a suburban community which had experienced no major crimes in the last ten years, she never felt safe, even behind locked doors. Second, she could not simply enjoy her husband and daughters without concern for their future. Third, and most problematically, she could not release herself from the past for fear that would mean abandoning and dishonoring her parents and those who had died. She lived either in fear of tomorrow or in the horror of yesterday.

As she explored her bind, she acknowledged that on rare occasions, when playing games with her children or bicycle riding with her husband during vacations, she had indeed experienced some fleeting moments of sheer delight. Upon further investigation, she realized that during those special moments she had lived only in the present. Her major question: Could she live in the present without dishonoring her family and failing to be watchful about the future? She decided to try an experiment with family members even before she had unearthed all her fears and questions. At least with her children and her husband, she could choose to be present in the moment as much as possible. Within days, her life changed profoundly.

In a letter she wrote me soon after making that decision, she said, "When I stay conscious of wanting to really be there with my children, I know only joy and happiness. I thought God wanted me always to think about the past, but I know now that was just my game. Only when I stay present do I truly experience God. I can remember the past when it is useful. I will never forget and that's all I need to know. Being present is not forgetting; it's just being present!"

She released the ghosts of the past without losing the lesson. Rather than maintaining vigilance against the spectre of war, she embraced the promise of planetary peace by living her own peace. Most significantly, she chose happiness as the most precious gift she could give herself and her family.

We create limitations with obsolete concepts that do not serve us. "Keep your eye on the future in order to master it," we tell ourselves. We might say instead, "Be present, take care of the present and you will be taking care of the future." Another common idiom often repeated is: "Forget the past and you will be doomed to repeat it." Perhaps we might rewrite this: "Be present and thus be happy and you will have no reasons to repeat the past you do not want." The lessons of the past are just that—lessons of the past. The unfolding present is absolutely unique in its circumstances and opportunities. If we choose to hold on to our unhappiness (and unhappy memories) from the past, we do not serve the present. Unhappiness is akin to confusion. By holding on to old discomforts, we bury the present and its wonder in the fog of the past.

Like the dedicated psychiatric analyst, we could try to dissect each event and circumstance of our personal history and those of our culture. We could rehash the situations of our early childhood in the hope of finding some useful insights. Perhaps some might surface. However, in the course of such a pursuit, by our design and our focus, we begin to make our past the present. What a strange process! Although we might suggest that such a journey has some historical value, we miss the essential point. *We are not in pursuit of history; we are in pursuit of happiness.*

As a veterinarian, Charles surprised himself constantly by the many different applications he found for utilizing the attitude of choosing happiness in his life and in his practice. He inspired his associates and assistants to develop new personal visions of interaction and service, with profound results. He credited the adoption of an open, nonjudgmental perspective as the key to innovation, daring business decisions and the spectacular growth of his clinic. Although all the shortcuts to happiness had had great impact on his daily living, none had been so useful to him this year as deciding to be present.

It is customary in his industry for veterinarians to cover the practices of colleagues during vacations. Once a year, Charles substituted for Dr. Daniels, an elderly physician who hated to do surgery and, therefore, left Charles with a rigorous surgical schedule in his absence. Any operations at Daniels's animal hospital would include the services of his assistant, a middle-aged woman named Freda who had deep religious convictions that included playing endless tapes of sermons of hellfire and brimstone as well as church music.

On the very first day, Charles had been slated to perform a hysterectomy on Mrs. Schreewater's one-hundred-pound prized rottweiler named Fang. The expensive dog was a mountain of muscle, with a bulging chest, neck, forelegs and a mouthful of snarling teeth. Clearly, Fang did not like veterinary clinics and expressed her displeasure by barking and growling. Once the dog had been caged by an attendant, Freda prepared the operating room while mumbling loudly "God be with us and watch over us." Freda did not like Fang. As Charles injected the anesthetic into the dog, Freda prayed "God, please don't let Fang have too much anesthetic!" Choir music and chants droned in the background. Instead of being distracted by the audio bombardment and by Freda's fearful comments, Charles decided to simply focus on the delicate job of completing the injection of anesthetic and monitoring Fang's response. Once again, Freda moaned "God protect her" as they shuttled Fang into surgery. They hooked the dog to an antiquated anesthesia machine which applied a continuous flow of gas to keep the animal sedated.

Once the effect of the anesthetic appeared fully in place, Charles made his incision into Fang's belly. As some blood began to flow, Freda said, "Dr. Daniels' patients never bleed." Charles smiled, thinking humorously that Dr. Daniels probably never did surgery since he went to such lengths to avoid it. Suddenly, Fang moaned and began to struggle on the table. Freda's eyes bulged as Fang's intestines popped out of her abdominal cavity and spilled over the table . . . all thirty feet of them. She shrieked, "God save us" and fell to the floor in prayer beneath Charles's feet. With a sermon from the stereo system now blaring into his ears, Charles tried to coax this woman to assist him quickly, but she stayed fixed in her position. He tried desperately to hold Fang with one hand while replacing her intestines with the other.

Obviously, the outdated anesthesia machine had not been giving the correct amount of gas to the dog. In this seemingly helpless, hopeless moment, Charles asked himself how he got into this preposterous situation. He imagined malpractice suits and skyrocketing liability insurance premiums. His thought process exploded with a confusing variety of conflicting concerns. Suddenly, he cut the inner dialogue as he remembered the gift of deciding to be present . . . in the present moment, he knew he could be happy and more useful in the face of these rapidly progressing events.

Charles focused one hundred percent of his attention immediately on the dog. His vision seemed sharper and his ability to think cleared. He restricted Fang's movement masterfully with one hand while using his teeth to remove the surgical glove from his other hand. Then, still holding the dog, he stretched his body and reached to the opposite end of the table and managed to adjust the machine to feed the animal more gas. Within moments he could feel Fang relaxing back onto the table. He replaced her intestines back into her abdominal cavity and completed the operation successfully while Freda continued her incantations on the floor. Charles whistled as he sutured the wound, realizing that being present had obliterated his fears, enhanced his ingenuity and skills and allowed him to convert an unfolding catastrophe into an easy, relaxed and satisfying experience.

He laughed as he told me this story, saying "Bears, if I could do this, then anything is possible!"

Our focused attention greatly enhances the power and pleasure of any event as well as our ability to handle and draw lessons from it. When someone speaks, we can look at her directly and listen to her words (rather than anticipate what we might say next or focus inward on other thoughts), thus amplifying our appreciation and understanding of her commentary as well as honoring her attempt to communicate with us. When brainstorming resolutions to problems or developing ideas for future ventures, we can set aside time to put the process on center stage in order to view and grasp each thought completely. When dining, we can take some moments in silence to view, smell and taste each bite, making the eating of every tiny morsel of food a satisfying and fulfilling experience rather than relying on quantity to create satisfaction and fullness.

When walking down a street, we can attend to the buildings, traffic and people we pass, thereby enhancing our safety as well as our enjoyment of the planet's creatures and creations. When making love, we can put other worldly concerns aside and heighten our moment-to-moment sense of touch, smell, sensuality and movement so we can express our caring fully. When selling merchandise to a customer, we can value their presence by listening attentively and respectfully to their wants and concerns so we can be more effective and helpful in meeting their needs (which serves them and, ultimately, serves us by enhancing the saleability and profitability of our endeavor). When teaching an employee or student, we can throw ourselves fully into communicating each detail of a procedure (as if nothing in the world exists in this moment except the job at hand) and be conscientious in allowing and answering questions that would enable the other person to be more successful in executing our instructions and delivering what we want.

When playing with a child, we can jump into the game with total enthusiasm, allowing our spontaneous, curious self to surface. When exercising, we can focus on each muscle and each movement, attentive to the miracle of our bodies and our abiding desire to make our bodies work healthfully.

We have only to remind ourselves to attend to each unfolding moment in our chosen endeavors. Being present not only increases our skill and effectiveness in personal and global relationships, business, child rearing and the like; it expands profoundly the depth and scope of each experience. A further benefit, perhaps the most spectacular of all, will be happiness!

Most of us have five senses (some might argue that we have more). A few of us, as the result of accident, disease or genetics, might be blessed with only four or three or even less. However, whether we ingest the world through sight, sound, touch, taste or smell, the unfolding universe moves by us and through us as a moment-to-moment current. Letting go of the past and future is diving into the current. Such a decision is neither irresponsible nor risky. Being present opens the doorway to happiness.

Shortcut # 5—Being Grateful

A personality characteristic that people clearly display when they become happier is their unending sense of gratitude. Although they might have expended much effort in their individual journeys toward increased clarity and comfort, most find that a sustained experience of happiness goes beyond their dreams. Even as I continue to walk the path, trying to be happier and more loving, I never cease to be awed by the blessing of inner peace I have been able to engender thus far. The gift looms larger than any effort I could have made to attain it. Being happy brings not only a recognition and harnessing of the power of our inner guidance, but also an acknowledgment of the synergistic power of a user-friendly universe that makes such happiness and self-trust possible.

When we are happy, we are truly grateful. The reverse also holds true. When we are grateful, we are truly happy. In fact, oftentimes I call gratitude the sweetest way to embrace happiness. We can cut through all the misery by turning our attention to being grateful. In spite of all the catastrophes that might occur, we can find in little and big ways bottomless wellsprings for our thankfulness. Gratitude then becomes the shortest of shortcuts to happiness.

Before proceeding further, we would do well to deal first with what might feel like a "natural" human propensity to resist gratitude and appreciation. The following story illustrates how we might develop such a propensity.

Recently I attended a birthday party given for a friend of my son Tayo. As soon as the little girl opened my son's gift, her mother leaned over and whispered into her ear, "Now, what do you say to Tayo?"

In a perfunctory manner, the child verbalized a stiff "Thank you" without even smiling or glancing at the gift giver.

The mother interceded. "I think you can do better than that," she said.

The little girl looked up at Tayo, grinned a plastic grin and said loudly, "Thank you." In a matter of seconds, her grin evaporated as she turned to unwrap the next gift.

By ritualizing the daughter's "thank you," the mother stripped it of its intended meaning. She short-circuited any appreciation this youngster might have been able to experience by the "have to" of a rather formal and mechanical response. She could have stimulated the little girl's gratitude by helping her understand all the energy Tayo had put into the gift giving. Not only had he spent almost an hour drawing elaborate cartoonlike figures on a four-page card, but he had searched several stores before locating a game which he believed she wanted. He purchased the gift using funds he had accumulated by babysitting, raking leaves, washing cars and the like. Later, when someone recounted the story behind Tayo's gift to the birthday girl, she smiled at him in amazement, then hugged him spontaneously. She voiced no mechanical "thank you" this time; her embrace expressed her genuine appreciation.

Perhaps most of us have been reared with the "should" of "thank you." Perhaps we have said these words so often without sincere appreciation that they stand devoid of any deep feelings. How often I have heard both adults and children declare, "I don't have to say 'Thank you.' " Or, "I don't want to say 'Thank you.' " For many of us, the expression remains polluted by childhood associations. No wonder we have become such an ungrateful lot! Not only do we resist feeling appreciation, we refrain from expressing it for strategic and tactical reasons. If we say "Thank you," do we now owe something in return? If we express our gratitude for help, does that diminish us? Suppression of such feelings for reasons of self-protection is an illusion. We gain nothing by our silence and stoicism. We do not cheat the world with our lack of gratitude; we cheat only ourselves.

Some people learn to simply mouth expressions of gratitude and, in the process, fail to reap the full harvest. Perhaps that was always the problem with the obligatory "thank you." Words! Though they could have been meaningful and expressive, they did not encourage us to make our gratitude an action. A smile begins to do it. A hug amplifies the feeling.

A helping hand or meaningful support makes gratitude even more tangible. In no way do our actions minimize the silent gratitude we might feel while viewing a sunset or watching puppies cuddle with their mother. To be grateful means not only to delight, enjoy and appreciate, but also to recognize simultaneously the blessing and the wonder of an experience. In such moments there is only happiness.

Yes, we might affirm that we have had special experiences of awe and wonder. We can immediately recognize such awesome and spectacular events as a birth, a Beethoven symphony, the panorama of the Grand Canyon as seen from the canyon rim, the first human steps on the moon, a kidney transplant or the heroic deed of one person helping another. However, we often fail to recognize the amazing events worthy of gratitude that occur all around us in each moment of every day.

Some people open their arms wide and say, "Oh, I am grateful to be alive!" or "I am grateful for the planet, the universe and everything in it!" With one sweep of their arms, they sum up all their feelings. In doing so, they miss the true glory of gratitude. In our teaching of the Option Process®, we encourage people always to be very specific in their explorations and to look beneath the abstractions and generalizations. Therefore, if someone speaks about discomfort, we ask for concrete examples of anxieties or annoyances. This perspective applies equally to experiences of gratitude.

We can train ourselves to be sensitive to the many miracles of living. In the face of such awareness, gratitude (and happiness) will bubble easily to the surface. As I sit here, I can think, see and breathe, all rather effortlessly. Incredible! My heart continues to pump, sustaining my life and my consciousness. What an amazing machine! How grateful I am that my fingers glide along the keys of this typewriter so that I can put these words on paper. Even the paper itself, made from the pulp of trees in giant mills, appears to be a miracle. By absorbing ink onto its surface, this white paper will hold my thoughts in frozen suspension so that I can one day share these ideas with others. How grateful I am for the lamp that allows me to see more clearly as I work, and how appreciative I am for the electricity that lights and heats the room I occupy. Ah! I can even view the dictionary, sitting near the edge of my desk, through the eyes of wonder! The glass of the window facing me protects me from the cold, yet affords me an expansive view of the sky. Truly amazing! I perceive so many marvels in my life when I become specific in my gratitude that I could not reasonably hope to catalogue them all.

Whenever we think we have lost our way or have noticed joy to be absent from our daily endeavors, we can look around and find a host of things, events or people to appreciate. If we make the items specific, we will never exhaust the resources with which to fuel our gratitude. A bird gliding on a warm summer breeze is no more miraculous than the wonder of a functioning toilet that supports our hygiene and health. The sand castle built by a child along the seashore is no more awesome than a computer printout which helps us track our finances. A quartz stone can be an object of delight, but so can the metal key which opens and locks our door. We tend to be stingy and discriminatory with our appreciation. But we can widen our vision. We can reserve the expression of gratitude for special occasions: Thanksgiving, a birthday, a marriage, a birth, an accident avoided. Or, we can be lavish with our thankfulness and, therefore, lavish with our happiness.

Probably a day does not go by when I have not told at least three or four of my six children how grateful I am for their presence in my life. I can't think it enough or say it enough! Our blessings come to life through our awareness.

A sales manager who attended one of our programs empowered her decision to be grateful with a resolution. She would write at least three notes every day to either clients or those in her own sales force to express sincere gratitude for their support and kindness. Her coworkers named her "Inspiration Annie." Those five minutes at the start of each day enabled her to experience her own delight; the gift of her energy has also inspired those working for her to put themselves on the line each month and exceed stated sales goals.

A chiropractor who loved the idea of implementing instant change in his life by making a decision or by revising his world vision began his personal transformation by thanking his patients, each individually, when they entered his treatment room. Then he asked them to take a moment to thank their bodies for supporting them and their life endeavors before he did any chiropractic adjustments. As a result, people relaxed more during his manipulations and no longer resisted the gentle prodding of what he now called his "happy hands." That one choice converted into action recast the texture of all his professional interactions and inspired him to enlist his patients to assist in their own healing.

An elementary school teacher, using a design she learned here at our teaching center, gathered her class into a gratitude circle. All the children were invited to express appreciation for a person or an event and to make that appreciation concrete and clear by sharing specific details. Initially, many students had to think for several moments, sometimes even minutes, before they could locate something in their lives for which they could be grateful. Now, these weekly sessions have become one of the more lively and happy activities in the class. Some students use the time to express appreciation for each other. Others now have their families doing gratitude circles at the dinner table.

We can discover an endless array of objects, circumstances and people to appreciate. We begin by making a simple choice to become aware and thankful. We can further heighten our experience by making our gratitude an action by saying or doing something to make our feelings visible!

A man who had participated in one of our seminars told us how the notion of being grateful had changed profoundly an experience which would have previously devastated him. He received a phone call informing him that his mother had just died. He had felt closer to her than anyone else in all the world. As he drove home to be with his father and brothers, he began to cry, mourning his loss. His world seemed shattered and empty. He wanted to scream his protest! But then he remembered the idea of invoking gratitude even in the most difficult of circumstances. He decided he could experiment, even in this moment. He paused for a second and searched his memory for just one recollection he could appreciate. Suddenly, he recalled the time, when he was eleven years old, when his mother helped him dress for a costume party. He had felt so appreciative then, and now, decades later, he felt so grateful again. Then he remembered all the summer afternoons at the lake when his mom had volunteered to be his swimming instructor. His lifelong love of the water had come from her delight in swimming. The gift of her input awed him. Only three short years ago, she had counseled him patiently during his painful divorce, never blaming him or his former wife for the separation. He had admired her neutrality. There were blemishes, too, on some of his memories. Sometimes, for example, she had been impatient and quick to anger. But he always felt she cared. His face stretched into a broad smile. He just loved her cream pies and the special cornbread she used to make on Sunday mornings. His laughter filled the car as he realized the special bridge that food had made between him and his mother.

Now at peace with his mother's death, he arrived at his parents' home beaming with joy and love. His family and friends greeted him with tear-stained, agonized faces. He decided to make his gratitude concrete by taking family and friends into the living room and telling touching as well as hilarious stories about his mother and himself. The cloud of mourning began to lift. As he encouraged others to share their stories and their gratitude, what had begun as a sorrowful gathering in the face of death turned into a celebration of one woman's life by those who loved her.

Gratitude! We can find it anyplace. We can invoke the feeling any time. We can make it concrete by sharing our appreciation with others. So if we become uncomfortable in any given moment, we can look at a flower, a pebble in the street or the tire on our car and be grateful. We can gaze at a person in the distance or at a cloud in the sky and be appreciative. We can smile at a stranger, hug someone we know or tidy a disorganized shelf and be thankful for the opportunity. If we choose gratitude, we will be happy!

Shortcut # 6—Deciding to Be Happy

This shortcut encompasses all the other shortcuts and could render them obsolete as we learn to empower our decisions. Deciding to prioritize happiness, to be authentic, present, grateful and nonjudgmental are, in essence, just different ways of deciding to be happy. They can also be helpful "practices" that we can implement with ease and effectiveness now. We can use them to create happiness and peace in our lives instantly and to simultaneously build happiness arcs in place of misery roadways. As we become happier, the pathways or shortcuts to happiness will, ultimately, become natural expressions of our evolving state of mind. Happier people tend to be authentic, present, grateful and nonjudgmental.

By deciding to be happier (to dispense with our unhappiness), we acknowledge our capacity to choose our beliefs and feelings as well as to take a directorial role in guiding our responses to events and people with a clear and conscious intention. Changing ourselves by decision reminds us that we can go directly to the experience of happiness and love. We can create a reason, like gratitude, to put ourselves in such an internal place (how wonderful!) or, in a manner of speaking, we can go to the head of the class and claim the experience we want. Although we have grown accustomed to creating happiness in response to favorable events or interactions, no stimulus is actually required.

We can empower the decision to be happy by reversing patterns of previous decisions each time we say *no* to unhappiness. When people do dialogues, they jettison unhappy beliefs, exposing comfort and ease beneath. It is as if we were happiness, love and joy camouflaged and compromised by layers of distrust and discomfort. Deciding to be happy is deciding to slice through these seemingly impenetrable layers of distrust and discomfort and to champion what we want to experience now. The moment we say "we can't, it's too difficult, we need more time," we create a self-fulfilling prophesy and find the act of changing ourselves either impossible, difficult or requiring much more time to accomplish. However, if we re-design our vision to live by and "make up" the belief we can do it now, in a single moment of time, then we precipitate a completely different reality to inhabit. We observe people demonstrating this possibility all the time. If they believe they require dialogues to change, then they use the dialogues to change and, certainly, that's a wondrous event. However, if they choose to believe they can just decide, then they just decide to be happy quickly and easily in spite of the circumstances and evidence, and we are left breathless and cheering for this possibility anyone can access.

Most of us expect our lives to have some minutes or hours or days or perhaps even weeks or months of discomforts because we have been taught systematically to use unhappiness as a strategy to motivate and protect ourselves and others. However, we can un-teach ourselves in an instant and begin anew. Just say *no* to unhappiness! If we choose not to believe a supposed crisis or problem will be bad for us, that's saying no to unhappiness. If we drop our judgments of someone we see as an adversary, that's saying no to unhappiness. If we decide not to use anger to move our friends, coworkers or those we love, that's saying no to unhappiness. These are examples of simple decisions which say *no* to unhappiness— and *yes* to happiness.

In deciding to be happy, we cut through to the heart of who we are. We want it! We can do it! And we will do it now! We can make this our clear intention—not a "should" or "must" or "have to" or a prescription for anyone else to fulfill. Although this might not be the preferred choice of many people on this planet right now, this can, nevertheless, be accomplished by any of us who make this our dedication. *To love is to be happy with ourselves and others (to accept ourselves and others).* Happiness makes love tangible! If we ever hope to create for ourselves a family, a community, a country and a world filled with people who are more loving, accepting, peaceful and supportive of each other, we must first give the gift of happiness (and love) to ourselves. We cannot reach out to give something we have not yet experienced inside.

However, we can seek and create happiness in itself and for itself. We don't need a reason to be happy. Making up reasons is part of the game we play when justifying unhappiness. I could decide to be happy, profoundly and sincerely happy (loving, open, comfortable, peaceful) for the next full minute. Why? Because I want to be profoundly and sincerely happy for sixty seconds. I could decide to extend my happiness for an entire hour or day or week or month or year or decade. Why? Because it pleases me to live in happiness and love and to greet my spouse or lover, parent, child, friend, coworker, acquaintance or any other creature, human or animal, with appreciation and delight.

What happens, someone might ask, if for some reason I want to jump off this happiness train after I have climbed aboard? No problem. We can always choose (decide) to be uncomfortable again—for happiness is a choice and misery is always an option.

If we go with the longing inside, we will choose happiness, and these simple tools, these shortcuts, will grease the wheels that will speed us on our way.

A Simple Blueprint
for Personal and Planetary Peace.

THE SHORTCUTS TO HAPPINESS

SHORTCUT #1—MAKING HAPPINESS *THE*
PRIORITY!

SHORTCUT #2—PERSONAL AUTHENTICITY

SHORTCUT #3—LETTING GO OF JUDGMENTS

SHORTCUT #4—BEING PRESENT

SHORTCUT #5—BEING GRATEFUL

SHORTCUT #6—DECIDING TO BE HAPPY

Postscript: The Celebration

Although we search to help ourselves and others embrace the blessings of happiness, we never make unhappiness an enemy during our pursuit. We can be happy in one moment, then absolutely miserable in the next. Isn't that amazing? What personal power! If I could conclude this book with one emphatic thought, it would be to suggest we befriend our unhappiness. We each do the best we can based on our current beliefs. We have the best of intentions even as we give ourselves grief. We do not have to condemn what we do in order to strive for more. Not judging our discomforts will change them forever and will free us to more easily create a happier lifestyle.

We are all amazing creatures in an amazing universe. We live endless blessings that often go unrecognized. Happiness, for Samahria, myself and those who have walked this road with us, has been the most empowering and enriching experience of our lives, enabling all of us to honor, acknowledge and celebrate the beauty, the love and the wonder of living. Additionally, we recognize we have only just begun.

We have, at times, been accused of being unrealistic in our hope and optimism because of our enthusiasm and delight in helping ourselves and others try to expand the walls of the human laboratory inside each of us. We feel privileged to have watched so many individuals dare to do the seemingly impossible in their lives and then reach out to others with happiness and love. As I have endeavored to share in this book, the results are tangible and visible in deeds and action.

Since it all begins with making one decision or one change, we could call this the ONE STEP program to happiness, love, peace and self-acceptance. One decision turned into action can get us there right now! One decision taken with energy and enthusiasm can change our internal world instantly and tap extraordinary personal power within, which inherently begins to change the external world we live in to become a more peaceful one—simply because we are each more peaceful ourselves.

Any single step opens the door. We can change our personal vision so that what we think and see works for us rather than against us. We can invoke the happiness option and access a user-friendly universe. We can drop our self-imposed limits and stretch into our dreams. Why not consider that anything might be possible? Peace of mind. World peace. People loving people. Happiness now.

We can stand on the edge of this opportunity and wish or we can jump into the heart of the matter. Prioritize happiness in this moment! Be authentic with ourselves and others! Jump into the present moment by fully attending, without reservation, to the people and events in our lives. Get in touch with being grateful for something! Drop a judgment today! Drop two judgments! Experiment with dropping them all. Decide to be happy and loving by just saying no to unhappiness and the beliefs which fuel it! Simple yet powerful choices! As happier and more loving people (not perfect, but on the road), we can enhance our own personal experiences dramatically and plant seeds that will change the world. We can talk this "talk" or we can walk this "talk." Actions bring this dream to life!

These are, indeed, times of miracles and wonder and they exist for any of us who choose to see the miracles and wonder.

One final note. These shortcuts to happiness have been synthesized from a diverse selection of possibilities. They represent the best of our understanding at this time. However, I am aware that as each of us chooses happiness and the spirit of our collective energies and choices mount, other useful shortcuts might become apparent. Some might be natural extensions of the ones itemized; others could cut new paths. We can use the six shortcuts to begin this life-enhancing and life-affirming attitudinal adventure, then continue to build our own repertoires.

Please share with me your insights into these shortcuts as well as any additional road signs or guideposts you discover along the way. Perhaps our pooled resources will birth the next installment of this unfolding adventure. You can write to me at the address below.

> With happiness and love and in celebration of you, me and the user-friendly universe,
>
> Bears (Barry Neil Kaufman)
>
> c/o The Option Institute & Fellowship
> P.O. Box 1180-H
> 2080 S. Undermountain Rd.
> Sheffield, MA 01257
> (413) 229-2100

References/
Additional Reading

This section is divided into two parts: the first is a page-noted reference listing of the more detailed examples and subjects I refer to; the second section is a brief alphabetical list of books that have tickled me and given me much delight. These books represent the cutting edge of evolving scientific and philosophical thought that support and help illuminate the principles of what we teach and the power of the attitude of love and acceptance.

References

PERSONAL NOTE

pp.6–7   Body chemistry: (If you change . . . cells of
           your body.) Deepak Chopra, M.D., *Quantum
           Healing*. Bantam, 1989.

CHAPTER II   **CREATING A PERSONAL VISION TO LIVE BY**

pp.33–34   National Institute for Neurological and Com-
           municative Disorders and Stroke (NINCDS):
           (During the last decade . . . slightest bodily
           disturbance.) Judith Hooper and Dick Teresi,
           Three Pound Universe. Macmillan, 1986.

39   Renewal of the body cells: (Ninety-eight per-
           cent of the atoms . . . fire in a second.) Deepak
           Chopra, M.D., *Quantum Healing*. Kenneth
           Jon Rose, *The Body In Time*. Wiley Science
           Editions, John Wiley & Sons, Inc., 1988.

45–46   Military language: (The following phrases
           . . . "permanent prehostility.") Sam Keen,
           Faces of the Enemy. Harper & Row, 1986.

61–62   Morphogenetic fields theory: (A contemporary biologist . . . easily and quickly.) Michael Talbot, *Beyond the Quantum*. Macmillan, 1987.

63   Plant and polygraph experiment: (In 1966 . . . plant life around him.) Roland Peterson, *Everyone Is Right*. DeVorss & Co., 1986.

CHAPTER III   THE HAPPINESS OPTION

pp.106–107   Sudden evolutionary changes: (Beetle fossils from . . . organisms occur suddenly.) Robert Augros and George Stanciu, *The New Biology*. New Science Library, Shambhala, 1987.

108–109   Thought and body chemistry: (—bodymind! . . . pop into existence.) Deepak Chopra, M.D., *Quantum Healing*.

CHAPTER IV   THRIVING IN A "USER-FRIENDLY" UNIVERSE

pp.123–24   Observable universe of expanding space: (Even the old vision . . . dance in space.) Dr. Michio Kaku and Jennifer Trainer, *Beyond Einstein*. Bantam, 1987. Paul Davies, *God and the New Physics.* Simon and Schuster, 1983; *Other Worlds.* Simon and Schuster, 1982. Arthur Eddington, *The Expanding Universe.* Cambridge University Press, 1933. Edward Harrison, *Masks of the Universe.* Macmillan, 1985.

126–27   The earth as Gaia: (Over twenty years . . . environment they inhabit.) James E. Lovelock, *Gaia: A New Look at Life on Earth.* Oxford University Press, 1979. "Gaia Hypothesis," *New York Times Science,* August 29, 1989.

128   Dutch scientist discovered synchronous rhythms: (In 1665, a Dutch . . . between the cells.) James Gleick, *Chaos.* Penguin, 1987.

130–33   Harmonious adaptation of species: (The black bears . . . shared the habitat.) R. Augros and G. Stanciu, *The New Biology.*

134   Hearing mechanism: (The ability to hear . . . music and so forth.) Fred Alan Wolf, *Body Quantum.* Macmillan, 1986.

CHAPTER V   NOTHING IS IMPOSSIBLE

pp.139–40   Brain defect cases: (A neurologist in England
. . . similar cases.) M. Talbot, *Beyond the
Quantum.*

140–42   Binary random generator/laws of probability:
(A professor at . . . to be helpful?) M. Talbot,
Beyond the Quantum.

142   Cardiology and remote healing: (A university
cardiologist . . . patients not included.) Blair
Justice, Ph.D., *Who Gets Sick.* Peak Press,
1987.

143–44   Our bodies and regeneration: (The bones in
our bodies . . . nature to run its course.) Robert
O. Becker, M.D., and Gary Selden, *The Body
Electric.* William Morrow and Co., 1985.

CHAPTER VI   SHORTCUTS TO HAPPINESS

pp.169–70   Amazing capacity of our dendrites: (However,
more sophisticated . . . density of our dendrites.) D. Chopra, M.D., *Quantum Healing.*
Richard Restak, M.D., *The Brain.* Bantam,
1984.

205 Revelations about the brain: (In the last two decades . . . parts as valid.) Sally P. Springer and Georg Deutsch, *Left Brain/Right Brain*. W.H. Freeman and Co., 1981. R. Restak, M.D., *The Brain*. J. Hooper and D. Teresi, *Three Pound Universe*.

206–207 Positron Emission Tomography (P.E.T.): (An instrument of . . . during different operations.) R. Restak, M.D., *The Brain*. B. Justice, Ph.D., *Who Gets Sick*. J. Hooper and D. Teresi, *Three Pound Universe*.

207 Brain experiments: (In one experiment . . . comfort and happiness.) R. Restak, M.D., *The Brain*. S.P. Springer and G. Deutsch, *Left Brain/Right Brain*.

212–13 Career counselors and questioning judgments: (Two professional career . . . lucrative new jobs.) Judith A. Dubin and Melanie R. Keveles, *Fired For Success*. Warner Books, 1990.

Additional Reading

Agros, Robert, and Stanciu, George. *The New Biology*. Boston: Shambhala, 1987.

Bach, Richard. *Illusions*. New York: Delacorte Press/Eleanor Friede, 1977.

Becker, Robert O., M.D. *Cross Currents*. Los Angeles: Tarcher, 1990.

Becker, Robert O., M.D., and Selden, Gary. *The Body Electric*. New York: William Morrow & Co., 1985.

Chopra, Deepak, M.D. *Quantum Healing*. New York: Bantam Books, 1989.

Davies, Paul. *God and the New Physics*. New York: Simon & Schuster, 1984.

———. *Other Worlds*. New York: Simon & Schuster, 1982.

Dubin, Judith A., and Keveles, Melanie R. *Fired For Success*. New York: Warner Books, 1990.

Dychtwald, Ken, Ph.D. *Age Wave*. New York: Bantam Books, 1990.

Dyer, Wayne, Ph.D. *Your Erroneous Zones*. New York: Funk and Wagnalls, 1976.

———. *What Do You Really Want For Your Children?* New York: Avon, 1986.

Gleick, James. *Chaos*. New York: Penguin, 1987.

Harrison, Edward. *Masks of the Universe.* New York: Macmillan, 1985.

Hooper, Judith, and Teresi, Dick. *Three Pound Universe.* New York: Macmillan, 1986.

Jampulsky, Gerald G., M.D. *Teach Only Love.* New York: Bantam Books, 1984.

———, and Cirincione, Diane V. *Love Is the Answer.* New York, Bantam Books, 1990.

Justice, Blair, Ph.D. *Who Gets Sick.* New York: Peak Press, 1987.

Kaku, Michio, Ph.D., and Trainer, Jennifer. *Beyond Einstein.* New York: Bantam, 1987.

Keen, Sam. *Faces of the Enemy.* New York: Harper & Row, 1986.

Lovelock, James. *Gaia: A New Look At Life On Earth.* New York: Oxford University Press, 1979.

Peterson, Roland. *Everyone Is Right.* Marina del Rey, CA: DeVorss & Co., 1986.

Restak, Richard, M.D. *The Brain.* New York: Bantam, 1984.

Rose, Kenneth Jon. *The Body In Time.* New York: John Wiley & Sons, Inc., 1988.

Sheldrake, Rupert. *The Presence of the Past.* New York: Times Books, 1988.

Siegel, Bernie, M.D. *Love, Medicine and Miracles.* New York: Harper & Row, 1986.

———. *Peace, Love and Healing.* New York: Harper & Row, 1989.

Simonton, O. Carl, Matthews-Simonton, Stephanie, and L. Creighton, James. *Getting Well Again.* New York: Bantam, 1980.

Springer, Sally P., and Deutsch, Georg. *Left Brain/Right Brain.* New York: Freeman & Co., 1989.

Stoff, Jesse A., M.D., and Pelligrino, Charles R., Ph.D. *Chronic Fatigue Syndrome.* New York: Random House, 1988.

Talbot, Michael. *Beyond the Quantum.* New York: Macmillan, 1987.

Wolf, Fred Alan. *Body Quantum.* New York: Macmillan, 1986.

Index

About the Author

BARRY NEIL KAUFMAN teaches a uniquely self-accepting and empowering process (The Option Process®), which has both educational and therapeutic applications. He and his wife, Samahria, are co-founders and co-directors of The Option Institute and Fellowship (P.O. Box 1180, 2080 S. Undermountain Rd., Sheffield, MA 01257, (413) 229-2100) which offers programs for people either challenged by adversity or trying to improve the quality of their lives. The Kaufmans, with their staff, also counsel individuals, couples, and families. Additionally, Mr. Kaufman lectures at universities, presents motivational talks, guides workshops and seminars, and has appeared in mass media throughout the country.

As a result of their innovative and successful program, The Son-Rise Program that they developed for their once-autistic child, the Kaufmans also counsel and instruct families wanting to create home-based teaching programs for their own special children. They teach professionals in this area as well.

Mr. Kaufman has written eight books, co-authored two screenplays with his wife (winning the coveted Christopher Award twice and also the Humanitas Prize), and has had articles featured in major publications. Barry Neil Kaufman's eighth and latest book, *Happiness Is a Choice,* is the most inspiring and hopeful statement of his work to date, a blueprint of simple, concrete methods to empower the decision to be happy. In *Happiness Is a Choice,* he pulls together the best of his twenty years' experience helping tens of thousands of people to achieve happiness.

His first book, *Son-Rise,* which details his family's inspiring journey with their once-autistic child, was dramatized as an NBC-TV special presentation. His subsequent books include *Giant Steps,* which details intimate and uplifting portraits of young people he has worked with and touched during times of extreme crisis. *To Love Is to Be Happy With* shares the specific applications of their nonjudgmental living. *A Miracle to Believe In* recounts the emotional and oftentimes miraculous story of the Kaufmans' teaching another family and group of volunteers to love themselves and, in turn, to love a little Mexican boy back to life. *The Book of Wows and Ughs* is a playful collection of sayings and insights. *A Land Beyond Tears,* co-authored with his wife, Suzi, presents a liberating approach to death and dying. *A Sense of Warning* details the Kaufmans' life-changing psychic experiences. His latest book, *Son-Rise: The Miracle Continues,* updates, expands and deepens the original *Son-Rise* story and details the journeys of other families who learned The Son-Rise Program and achieved extraordinary results with their own children.

For information on audio and video cassette tapes and books by the Kaufmans as well as program, workshop and lecture information, write: Option Indigo Press, P.O. Box 1180, Sheffield, MA 01257.